8 Secrets To Remember On Your Journey In Greatness
ISBN 978-0-692-17796-9 © 2021 by Paul J Nyamweya
8GreatSecrets.com

All scripture references are from the King James Version of The Bible unless otherwise indicated.

Scripture quotations marked AMP are taken from the Amplified Bible, Copyright © 1954, 1958, 1962, 1964, 1965, 1987 by The Lockman Foundation. Used by permission.

Scripture quotations marked MSG are taken from THE MESSAGE, copyright © 1993, 2002, 2018 by Eugene H. Peterson. Used by permission of NavPress, represented by Tyndale House Publishers. All rights reserved.

PRINTED IN THE UNITED STATES OF AMERICA

Table of Contents

Dedication

To The Lord God, The Most High; My Exceeding Abundantly Above All I Can Ask or Think Savior; My Ever Increasing Greatness Nurturer, Teacher And Mentor.

Acknowledgments

First and foremost, The Holy Spirit, for revealing to me the *Treasure* hidden in Isaiah 60:22 and *leading* me to put what I learned into a book so that it may be a blessing to others.

My late mother, Keziah Nyamweya, for *imparting* into my life a fear of and sensitivity to The Lord from a young age. Despite the fact that I did not fully embrace it at the time, the longer I live, the more thankful I am for her mentorship.

My late father, Justus Nyamweya, for pushing and *challenging* me to always strive to be the *best* I can be.

Pastor Kenneth Davis, for being a spiritual mentor in my life during my *formative* years as a young believer.

Dr. Mike Murdock, for your mentorship and *advocation* that every believer should *document* their persuasions and the thoughts God gives them. *God*

Sent His Son But Left His Book. The passion for writing was ignited, and the Seed that would later *germinate* into this book was planted, under the anointing of your ministry.

Deborah Murdock Johnson, for over ten years of valuable *mentorship* and *leadership* in creativity, writing, and publishing.

Paulette "Mum" Hollingsworth and Diane Irving, for being consistent and tireless *intercessors* in my life over the years.

Bruce "Jay" Hollingsworth and The G-Side Group, for constant and relentless *encouragement*.

Javier Rivera, for consistently showering me with *revelation* in every conversation we have. You are a real "jalapeno" in The Kingdom. Praise The Lord for the "And The Lord was with Joseph" discussions.

Benson Agbortogo, for issuing the *challenge*, "Leaders are readers, but writers are legacy builders."

Apostle Jackson, for speaking this book into existence years before it entered my heart or mind.

Prophet Richard Adu-Gyamfi, for spiritual nurturing, guidance, oversight, and covering, during this season of my life.

Prophet Samuel Ofori Boakye, for your intercession and encouragement that ushered this book to the finish line.

Archbishop-elect Salifu Amoako, for speaking a word that *amplified* the revelation and teaching grace in my life.

Prophet Gideon Baffoe, for saying a word that *accelerated* the completion of this book.

Bishop Noble Simpson for speaking a *blessing* of revelation and insight over my life.

Elizabeth Jaring for graphics *brilliance*.

Finally, Rochelle Walker, for divine insight and rich discussions that *preserved* and *protected* the book's integrity, excellence, and purity.

Isaiah 60:22

"A little one...

shall become...

a thousand...

and a small one...

a strong nation:

I the Lord...

will hasten it...

in His time."

Introduction

Everything Starts Small.

Two thousand years before the birth of Christ, God called an older man in his seventies and told him He would make of him *a great nation.*

"Now the Lord had said unto Abram, Get thee out of thy country, and from thy kindred, and from thy father's house, unto a land that I will shew thee: And I will make of thee **a great nation**, and I will bless thee, and make thy name great; and thou shalt be a blessing:

"And I will bless them that bless thee, and curse him that curseth thee: and in thee shall all families of the earth be blessed. So Abram departed, as the Lord had spoken unto him; and Lot went with him: and Abram was <u>seventy and five years old</u> when he departed out of Haran." (Genesis 12:1-4).

Two and a half decades later, God revisited Abram to remind him of His promise.

"And when Abram was <u>ninety years old and nine</u>, the Lord appeared to Abram, and said unto him, I am the Almighty God; walk before Me, and be thou perfect. And I will make My covenant between Me and thee, and will **multiply thee exceedingly.**

"And Abram fell on his face: and God talked with him, saying, As for Me, behold, My covenant is with thee, and thou shalt be **a father of many nations.** Neither shall thy name any more be called Abram, but thy name shall be Abraham; for **a father of many nations** have I made thee. And I will make thee **exceeding fruitful**, and I will **make nations of thee**, and **kings shall come out of thee**," (Genesis 17:1-6).

When God first visited him, he was already well past the years when a man would typically think of *starting* a family. Yet, two and half decades later, God still reiterated His initial promise.

If It Is Difficult To Believe You Can Have A Child At 75, How Much Harder Would It Be To Believe You Can Have One At 99?

Have You Been Tempted To "Help" God?

In previous decades, Sarai *struggled* with seeing how the prophecy would be fulfilled. When she looked at her circumstances, she must have *wondered* how it would come to pass. The years were passing by, and still, there was no conception. She decided to "help" God by offering her handmaid to her husband.

"Now Sarai Abram's wife bare him no children: and she had an handmaid, an Egyptian, whose name was Hagar. And Sarai said unto Abram, Behold now, the Lord hath <u>restrained</u> me from bearing: I pray thee, <u>go in unto my maid</u>; it may be that I may <u>obtain children by her</u>. And Abram hearkened to the voice of Sarai," (Genesis 16:1-2).

No Substitute Can Give You What God Will

Going Ahead of God Has Consequences.

Sarai ended up battling *insecurities*.

When she approached Abram to sleep with her maid, she was convinced God had *restrained* her from having children. The very thing that would *validate* her as a wife and fulfill the prophecy that had been given to her husband a decade earlier appeared to now rest on *another.*

"And Sarai Abram's wife took Hagar her maid the Egyptian, after Abram had dwelt ten years in the land of Canaan, and gave her to her husband Abram to be his wife. And he went in unto Hagar, and she conceived: and when she saw that she had conceived, her mistress was <u>despised in her eyes</u>," (Genesis 16:3-4).

Sarai's suggestion now appeared as a *threat* in her own eyes. Her recommendation now fueled her *insecurities.* Ultimately, she took it out on her handmaid, Hagar, who was now pregnant with Abram's child.

"And Sarai said unto Abram, My wrong be upon thee: I have given my maid into thy bosom; and when she saw that she had conceived, <u>I was despised in her eyes:</u> the Lord judge between me and thee. But Abram said unto Sarai, Behold, thy maid is in thy hand; do to her as it pleaseth thee. And when <u>Sarai dealt hardly with her, she fled from her face</u>," (Genesis 16:5-6).

However, God In His Mercy Still Stood By The Child Who Was Rightly A Seed of Abraham.

"And the angel of the Lord found her by a fountain of water in the wilderness, by the fountain in the way to Shur. And he said, Hagar, Sarai's maid, whence camest thou? and whither wilt thou go? And she said, I flee from the face of my mistress Sarai.

"And the angel of the Lord said unto her, Return to thy mistress, and submit thyself under her hands. And the angel of the Lord said unto her, I will **multiply thy seed exceedingly**, that it shall not be numbered for multitude.

"And the angel of the Lord said unto her, Behold, <u>thou art with child</u>, and <u>shalt bear a son</u>, and <u>shalt call his name Ishmael</u>; because the Lord hath heard thy affliction," (Genesis 16:7-11)

A Father of Many Nations

God gave Abram a new name, Abraham, to enforce his self-portrait as a father. God emphasized he was not only a father of one; *but a father of MANY nations.*

"And Abram fell on his face: and God talked with him, saying, As for Me, behold, My covenant is with thee, and thou shalt be **a father of many nations.** Neither shall thy name any more be called

Abram, but thy name shall be Abraham; for **a father of many nations** have I made thee. And I will make thee **exceeding fruitful**, and I will **make nations of thee**, and **kings shall come out of thee**," (Genesis 17:1-6).

God's conversations with Abraham were the exact opposite of what his circumstances suggested. By giving him a new name, God changed his self-portrait...his identity...the way he looked at himself; *so he could start looking at himself the way God looked at him.*

Your journey in Greatness will change the way you look at yourself. God already sees you as blessed. If you do not see yourself as blessed, you will not enjoy all the benefits of being blessed that God intends for you experience. *How you see yourself matters more than how God sees you.*

"And I will establish My covenant between Me and thee **and thy seed after thee in their generations** for an everlasting covenant, to be a God unto thee, **and to thy seed after thee.**

"And I will give unto thee, and **to thy seed after thee**, the land wherein thou art a stranger, **all the land of Canaan, for an everlasting possession;** and **I will be their God**," (Genesis 17:7-8).

Even before Abraham had a child with Sarai, God was already having conversations with him about his child's children...*his Seed's Seed.* God discusses the everlasting covenant He will have with them, including the land they will possess *while Sarai is still incapable of conceiving.*

The self-image of those walking alongside you on your journey will have to change. God changed Abram's name to Abraham, but he instructed Abraham to change Sarai's name to Sarah.

Your Self-Portrait Will Affect Others

Only by Abraham walking in his new identity, could he positively *influence* Sarah, formerly Sarai, to walk in *hers.*

"And God said unto Abraham, As for Sarai thy wife, thou shalt not call her name Sarai, but **Sarah shall her name be**.

"And I will bless her, and give thee a son also of her: yea, I will bless her, and **she shall be a mother of nations; kings of people shall be of her**," (Genesis 17:15-16).

How You See Yourself Will Ultimately Affect How Those Assigned To You Will See Themselves.

Even after Abraham received *unequivocal* promises related to his new identity and Sarai's adopted name, *he still had questions.* He *wondered* how a couple their age could have a child.

"Then Abraham fell upon his face, and laughed, and said in his heart, **Shall a child be born** unto him that is <u>an hundred years old</u>? and shall Sarah, that is <u>ninety years old</u>, bear?"

Abraham still thought God was referring to Ishmael. "And Abraham said unto God, <u>O that Ishmael might live before Thee</u>!" (Genesis 17:17-18).

The Lord then went a step further to reiterate that the Covenant Seed He had been describing would come from Sarah's womb.

"And Abraham said unto God, O that Ishmael might live before Thee! And God said, **Sarah thy wife shall bear thee a son** indeed; and thou shalt call his name Isaac: and **I will establish My covenant with him for an everlasting covenant, and with his seed after him**," (Genesis 17:18).

God Will Give You A New Confession

What You Keep Saying Determines What You Ultimately Believe.

What You Keep Saying Determines What Eventually Happens in Your Life.

"<u>Death and life</u> are in the power of the tongue and they that love it <u>shall eat the fruit</u> thereof," (Proverbs 18:21).

As God gave Abraham and Sarah their new names, He gave them a *different* confession.

Every time they introduced themselves to a stranger, they were essentially confessing, *"We are the father and mother of many nations."*

Every time they called out to each other, they were affirming, *"We are the father and mother of many nations."*

Every time someone in their household would call them by their new names...*that self-portrait was reinforced.*

The more they *responded* to their new names, the closer they got to the *manifestation* of the promise.

God gave Abraham instructions for the *establishment* of the "impossible" covenant He made with him. The instructions addressed Abraham's Seed's Seed...*those born of Sarah.*

Possible Instructions...
...Impossible Results

At the time, Abraham's Seed through Sarah did not even exist or even appear remotely possible...*yet God mentioned it explicitly.*

"And God said unto Abraham, Thou shalt <u>keep My covenant</u> therefore, **thou, and thy seed after thee in their generations**. This is My covenant, which ye shall keep, **between Me and you and thy seed after thee**; Every man child among you shall be circumcised.

"And ye shall circumcise the flesh of your foreskin; and <u>it shall be a token of the covenant betwixt Me and you</u>. And he that is eight days old shall be circumcised among you, **every man child in your generations**, he that is born in the house, or bought with money of any stranger, which is not of thy seed. **He that is born in thy house**, and he that is bought with thy money, must needs be circumcised: and <u>My covenant shall be in your flesh</u> for an everlasting covenant, (Genesis 17:9-13).

God even stipulated consequences for those within Abraham's household, *now and in the future*, who would not comply.

"And the uncircumcised man child whose flesh of his foreskin is not circumcised, that soul shall be <u>cut off from his people</u>; he hath broken My covenant," (Genesis 17:9-14).

At 99 years old, Abraham took a step of faith to *establish* the covenant between The Lord and him. The circumcision served as a *token* on his flesh of the covenant.

"And Abraham was <u>ninety years old and nine</u>, when he was <u>circumcised in the flesh of his foreskin</u>," (Genesis 17:24).

Which is easier? Believing God you can father a child at 99 years old or believing God you can have a child at 99 years old, after *circumcision*, after going through the *healing* process at that age, and then after *intimacy* with your wife once you have healed? Not to mention, *your wife* is 90 years old!

Your Journey In Greatness Will Require A Step of Faith.

God Will Repair Your Broken Places

Abraham cares for Ishmael as any father would. As he battles with the *impossibility* of Sarah having a child, he presents Ishmael to The Lord.

"Then Abraham fell upon his face, and laughed, and said in his heart, <u>Shall a child be born unto him that is an hundred years old? and shall Sarah, that is ninety years old, bear?</u> And Abraham said unto God, <u>O that Ishmael might live before Thee!</u>" (Genesis 17:17-18).

Ishmael, barely in his teens, is growing up in an environment where he is *unwelcome*.

His mother does not have the same rights and status as Sarah. All the circumstances surrounding his conception, birth, and early childhood, are bound to have brought *tension* within the household.

God Will Step In

God steps in...*defusing the tension.*

God steps in...*settling the ambiguity.*

"And as for Ishmael, I have heard thee: Behold, **I have blessed him**, and **will make him fruitful**, and **will multiply him exceedingly**; twelve princes shall he beget, and **I will make him a great nation**," (Genesis 17:20).

In His faithfulness, God addresses what brought *pain* in Abraham's home life during their *waiting* season. God had a *specific* word for Ishmael, the child born out of *impatience*.

God later switches the conversation from the child who could be seen, to the child who *could not be seen*. The "impossible" child will emerge from the "dead" womb.

Sarah's past identity, Sarai, *is ignored*.

She is now the *mother of many nations*. God even put *a time frame on the manifestation* of the promise, all the while referring to the child, Isaac, by name...*like he is a living being!*

"But My covenant will I establish <u>with Isaac</u>, which **Sarah shall bear** unto thee <u>at this set time in the next year</u>. And He left off talking with him, and God went up from Abraham," (Genesis 17:21-22).

Expect God To Visit You

Abraham recognized a moment of Divine visitation. "And the Lord appeared unto him in the plains of Mamre: and he sat in the tent door in the heat of the day; And he lift up his eyes and looked, and, lo, <u>three men stood by him: and when he saw them, he ran to meet them</u> from the tent door, and <u>bowed himself toward the ground</u>, And said, My Lord, <u>if now I have found favour in Thy sight, pass not away, I pray thee, from Thy servant:</u>" (Genesis 18:1-3).

Abraham *swiftly* served and attended to the Divine guests. He sowed the Seed of Hospitality. (See Genesis 18:4-7.)

After he served them, they asked him about his wife. They revisited the promise The Lord had given him. They addressed her as Sarah, *the mother of many nations.*

"And he took butter, and milk, and the calf which he had dressed, and <u>set it before them</u>; and he <u>stood by them under the tree, and they did eat.</u>

"And they said unto him, Where is Sarah thy wife? And he said, Behold, in the tent. And he said, I will certainly return unto thee according to the time of life; and, lo, **Sarah thy wife shall have a son.** And Sarah heard it in the tent door, which was behind him. Now Abraham and Sarah were <u>old and well stricken in age</u>; and it <u>ceased to be with Sarah after the manner of women</u>," (Genesis 18:8-11).

The Covenant Will Preserve Your Life

Even Sarah, his wife, *laughed* at the thought of having one child, let alone the concept of the two of them becoming *father and mother of many nations*.

"Therefore <u>Sarah laughed within herself</u>, saying, <u>After I am waxed old shall I have pleasure, my lord being old also?</u> And the Lord said unto Abraham, Wherefore did Sarah laugh, saying, Shall I of a surety bear a child, which am old?

"Is any thing too hard for the Lord? **At the time appointed I will return unto thee, according to the time of life, and Sarah shall have a son.** Then Sarah denied, saying, I laughed not; for she was afraid. And he said, Nay; but thou didst laugh," (Genesis 18:12-15).

Despite the fact Sarah *lied* to The Lord, *she lived to see the prophecy's fulfillment in her life* because of God's covenant with Abraham.

There was a time Abraham thought his heir would be the steward of his house. "After these things the word of the Lord came unto Abram in a vision, saying, Fear not, Abram: I am thy Shield, and thy Exceeding Great Reward. And Abram said, Lord God, what wilt Thou give me, seeing I go childless, and <u>the steward of my house is this Eliezer of Damascus</u>? And Abram said, Behold, to me Thou hast given no seed: and, lo, <u>one born in my house is mine heir</u>," (Genesis 15:2-3).

God responded by telling him his Seed will be as the sand on the seashore and the stars in the heavens. "And, behold, the word of the Lord came unto him, saying, This shall not be thine heir; but **he that shall come forth out of thine own bowels shall be thine heir.** And he brought him forth abroad, and said, Look now toward heaven, and tell **the stars**, if thou be able to number them: and he said unto him, **So shall thy seed be**," (Genesis 15:4-5).

It Did Not Happen Overnight

The Manifestation Took Time To Appear.

Yet, Abraham believed The Lord.

"And he <u>believed in the Lord</u>; and He <u>counted it to him for righteousness</u>," (Genesis 15:6).

"And He gave him the covenant of circumcision: and so Abraham **begat Isaac**, and circumcised him the eighth day; and Isaac **begat Jacob**; and Jacob begat **the twelve patriarchs**," (Acts 7:8).

"All the souls that came with Jacob into Egypt, which came out of his loins, **besides Jacob's sons' wives, all the souls were threescore and six**; And the **sons of Joseph**, which were born him in Egypt, were two souls: all the souls of the house of Jacob, which came into Egypt, were **threescore and ten**," (Genesis 46:26-27).

"And the children of Israel were **fruitful**, and **increased abundantly**, and **multiplied**, and **waxed exceeding mighty**; and **the land was filled with them**," (Exodus 1:7).

Your God-Given Promise May Not Materialize Overnight, But It Will Surely Come.

What Began With One Man, Would Eventually Create A Multitude of People.

A Worldwide Phenomenon

On March 10, 1876, a man fabricated a piece of equipment that allowed him to communicate with his assistant. That man was Alexander Graham Bell. The assistant, Watson.

Nowadays, it is almost unheard of to spend a day without using a telephone, or at least a variant of it in the form of the modern-day smartphone. It is even possible that you may be reading this book on your smartphone or listening to it via an app on your phone.

An invention that started with one person spread and is now commonplace.

At the writing of this book, there are almost as many cellphone subscriptions as people on the earth. **7 billion!**

What started with one person has now become a worldwide phenomenon.

In this book, I share a scripture that I contemplate often. I even write it on Offering envelopes when I sow my Tithe and Seed.

It is a scripture I revisit each time I evaluate where I am on my journey in Greatness.

You, Too, Are On Your Journey.

You, Too, Have Your Greatness.

Eight Secrets that will inspire and encourage you *in your Greatness* are hidden in this one chapter, Isaiah 60 and *summarized* in its last verse.

Isaiah 60:22 unveils ***8 Secrets To Remember On Your Journey In Greatness***.

"A little one **shall become a thousand**, and a small one **a strong nation**: I the Lord will hasten it in His time," (Isaiah 60:22).

"The smallest one **will become a thousand** (a clan), And the least one **a mighty nation**. I, the Lord, will quicken it in its [appointed] time," (Isaiah 60:22 AMP).

"The runt will become **a great tribe**, the weakling become **a strong nation**. I am God. At the right time I'll make it happen," (Isaiah 60:22 MSG).

Isaiah 60:22

"A little one...

    shall become...

        a thousand...

           and a small one...

                a strong nation:

                    I the Lord...

                        will hasten it...

                            in His time."

"A Little One..."
Isaiah 60:22

~ Secret #1 ~
Do Not Be Discouraged Because You Are Starting Small

"A little one..." (Isaiah 60:22).

Today Is Not Your Tomorrow!

Where you are Today is not where you have to be Tomorrow. What you are experiencing Today is not necessarily what you will experience Tomorrow.

Israel sinned against The Lord, so He delivered them into the hands of Midian for seven years. The Midianites *overpowered* them, so they *fled* to the dens in the mountains. There, they fortified themselves, living in caves, until the danger abated.

Initially, The Israelites were overrun by the Midianites; now, they had to face the Amalekites. All their crops were destroyed - no sheep, cattle, or donkeys remained. There was nothing left for the Israelites to eat.

Whenever Israel *planted* crops, the Midianites and Amalekites would *invade* them and *camp* in their fields.

The invaders arrived like a multitude of consuming grasshoppers; they and their livestock were *innumerable*. They came into the land to destroy it, and because of their assault, Israel became severely *poverty-stricken*. (See Judges 6:1-6.)

"And Israel was <u>greatly impoverished because of the Midianites</u>; and the children of Israel cried unto the Lord," (Judges 6:6).

An Unlikely Candidate

Gideon was a *nobody* when he experienced his heavenly visitation. Gideon had to thresh wheat in a winepress to hide it from his oppressors. He did not have the liberty to do this openly.

Gideon may have felt little, despised, rejected, insignificant, and helpless, yet the angel addressed him as "a mighty man of valor." The angel's conversation with him was not based on where he was at that moment in his life, but on where he was going...*where God was taking him.*

"And there came an angel of the Lord, and sat under an oak which was in Ophrah, that pertained unto Joash the Abi–ezrite: and his son Gideon threshed wheat by the winepress, to hide it from the Midianites.

"And the angel of the Lord appeared unto him, and said unto him, The Lord is with thee, thou mighty man of valour," (Judges 6:11-12).

Gideon did not accept being addressed as *a man of* courage. Gideon did not possess that same self-image. He never saw himself as a warrior. Instead, he decided to *educate the angel* on how miserable his life had become.

"And Gideon said unto him, Oh my Lord, if the Lord be with us, why then is all this befallen us? and where be all His miracles which our fathers told us of, saying, Did not the Lord bring us up from Egypt? but now the Lord hath forsaken us, and delivered us into the hands of the Midianites," (Judges 6:13).

The Hidden Snare...
...Called Blame

Gideon *blamed* God for their circumstances.

Every Time You Blame Another...You Leave Yourself Powerless.

Every Time You Blame Another...You Render Yourself Incapable of Change.

Every Time You Blame Another...You Seal Your Door of Options.

In a merciful stroke of genius, God *redirects* Gideon to the strength within him, *dispossessing* him of the ability to persist in blaming others. God *affirms* that the power Gideon carried was *sufficient* to bring about the deliverance Israel craved. God places a Divine mandate on Gideon's Assignment by *validating* that He is The One sending him.

"And the Lord looked upon him, and said, Go <u>in this thy might</u>, and <u>thou shalt save Israel from the hand of the Midianites</u>: have not <u>I sent thee</u>?" (Judges 6:14).

Inward Blame...
...Is Blame The Same

Since Gideon had no one else to find fault with, he decided to blame *himself*. He looked inward for ways to *disqualify* himself from the call. Gideon wanted to update God with a *comprehensive* report on his family history, place in society, and why he was *not* the right candidate.

"And he said unto Him, Oh my Lord, wherewith shall I save Israel? behold, <u>my family is poor</u> in Manasseh, and <u>I am the least in my father's house</u>," (Judges 6:15).

Gideon wanted to look at his Past to *discredit* his Future, but God looked at his Future and *ignored* his Past.

God Does Not Need Permission From Your Past To Determine Your Future.

You May Be Looking At Your Past To Discredit Your Future; Yet God Is Looking At Your Future and Ignoring Your Past.

An Experience With God Will Defy Any Attachment To Mediocrity

God *reaffirmed* His commitment to Gideon.

"And the Lord said unto him, Surely I will be with thee, and <u>thou shalt smite the Midianites as one man</u>," (Judges 6:16).

Though you may feel vulnerable Today, *you will not always be weak*. You can *defy* your circumstances. You can *disregard* the expectations of your critics.

A weakling Today can become a General Tomorrow. "Beat your plowshares <u>into swords</u>, and your pruninghooks <u>into spears</u>: let the weak say, **I am strong**," (Joel 3:10).

When Gideon ran out of personal excuses and arguments to refute the angel's words, he asked for the messenger to *validate* himself; a challenge that was *eagerly accepted*.

"And he said unto him, If now I have found grace in thy sight, <u>then shew me a sign</u> that thou talkest with me.

"And when <u>Gideon perceived that he was an angel of the Lord</u>, Gideon said, Alas, O Lord God! for because <u>I have seen an angel of the Lord face to face</u>," (Judges 6:17, 22).

Gideon was so *moved* by the experience that he built an altar there unto The Lord. There was no doubt in his heart that he had experienced a *Divine Visitation*.

"And the Lord said unto him, Peace be unto thee; <u>fear not: thou shalt not die.</u> Then <u>Gideon built an altar there</u> unto the Lord, and called it Jehovah-shalom: unto this day it is yet in Ophrah of the Abi-ezrites," (Judges 6:22-24).

Gideon's First Instruction

That same night, Gideon received *his first instruction* upon learning his identity as a mighty man of valor. God instructed him to *seize* his father's second seven-year-bull, *tear down* the altar of Baal that his father had built and *cut down* the Asherah fertility pole that had been fabricated beside it.

Gideon was to *build an altar* unto The Lord on top of the hill, present the prime bull as the burnt offering, and use the wood from the pole as the firewood. The clear message was Baal had no place there and that *The Lord was his God*.

Gideon followed The Lord's instructions under the cover of night because he was leery of his family and the people in the neighborhood who had pledged their allegiance to Baal.

"And it came to pass the same night, that the Lord said unto him, <u>Take thy father's young bullock</u>, even the second bullock of seven years old, and <u>throw down the altar of Baal</u> that thy father hath, and <u>cut down the grove that is by it</u>: And <u>build an altar unto the Lord thy God</u> upon the top of this rock, in the ordered place, and <u>take the second bullock</u>, and <u>offer a burnt sacrifice with the wood of the grove</u> which thou shalt cut down.

"Then Gideon took ten men of his servants, and did as the Lord had said unto him: and so it was, <u>because he feared</u> his father's household, and the men of the city, that he could not do it by day, that <u>he did it by night</u>," (Judges 6:25-27).

Your New Identity...Will Be Challenged

The next morning, the people woke up to a *demolished* Baal altar, their pagan pole *cut down*, a *new altar* in its place, with *a new sacrifice smoldering* on top of it.

A sacrifice not intended for Baal.

"And when the men of the city arose early in the morning, behold, <u>the altar of Baal was cast down</u>, and <u>the grove was cut down</u> that was by it, and the second <u>bullock was offered upon the altar that was built</u>," (Judges 6:28).

They woke up to *the showcasing of Gideon's new identity*, even though, at the time, they did not know he was responsible for *razing* the altar of Baal. Eventually, the news spread that Gideon had done it.

"And they said one to another, Who hath done this thing? And when they enquired and asked, they said, <u>Gideon the son of Joash hath done this thing</u>," (Judges 6:29).

Your New Identity...Will Be Defended

The city's men *demanded* Gideon's life in exchange for the damage he had done to the pagan shrine. Joash, Gideon's father, stepped in and *defied* them.

Gideon sacrificed his father's *prime* bull, yet his father *defended* him. Gideon destroyed his father's Baal altar, yet his father *stood up* for him.

"Then the men of the city said unto Joash, Bring out thy son, <u>that he may die</u>: because he hath <u>cast</u>

41

down the altar of Baal, and because he hath cut down the grove that was by it," (Judges 6:30).

Gideon's father placed vengeance in the hands of Baal. If Baal was worth anything, then indeed, *he can defend himself.* If Gideon's father was unwilling to reprimand his son for what he did, why would he let the crowd act? If Baal has any power, *he can fight his own battles.*

"And Joash said unto all that stood against him, Will ye plead for Baal? will ye save him? he that will plead for him, let him be put to death whilst it is yet morning: if he be a god, let him plead for himself, because one hath cast down his altar," (Judges 6:31).

The crowd stared *helplessly* at what Gideon had done. They, too, *echoed* the proclamation of the angel. They started calling Gideon by a new name. They began to *perceive* him as one who had *a new identity.* A *God-visitation* and a *God-instruction* caused a ripple in the fabric of the community's belief system.

"Therefore on that day he called him Jerubbaal, saying, Let Baal plead against him, because he hath thrown down his altar," (Judges 6:32).

A Private Visitation Culminated In A Public Demonstration.

Your Day of Visitation Is Here

Gideon experienced a Divine Visitation.

On that day, he *rejected the false deity*. He *cleansed* his environment of anything anti-God, anything that did not reflect his Future and the *identity* God had given him.

Are you feeling *despised...insignificant... rejected...unknown...or diminutive; a* dwarf relative to where you want to be in life? Remember, you received your Divine Visitation the day you *acknowledged* the Lord Jesus and *confessed* with your mouth that He died for your sins and rose again that you might have eternal life with God.

You received your Divine Visitation the day you *recognized* that Jesus Christ is The Son of The Living God.

"That if thou shalt <u>confess with thy mouth</u> the Lord Jesus, and shalt <u>believe in thine heart</u> that God hath <u>raised Him from the dead, thou shalt be saved</u>," (Romans 10:9).

You received your Divine Visitation the day you got *saved* and *surrendered* your life...*the day Jesus became your Lord and Savior.*

On that day, you became *a new creation.*

"Therefore if any man be in Christ, <u>he is a new creature</u>: old things are passed away; behold, <u>all things are become new</u>," (2 Corinthians 5:17).

Arise!

Shine!

Your Light has *come!*

The Glory of The Lord has *risen* on you!

The Lord Jesus Is That Light

"Arise, shine; for <u>thy Light is come</u>, and the Glory of <u>the Lord is risen upon thee</u>," (Isaiah 60:1-2).

Be *uplifted.*

Be *enlightened.*

The light you have been waiting to see...

The instruction you have been tarrying for...

The knowledge you have been craving...*is now coming to you.*

The insight you desperately hunger for...*is entering your life.*

God's Glory will *overshadow* any impending darkness on the earth.

God's Glory Shall Be Seen On Your Life

"For, behold, the darkness shall cover the earth, and gross darkness the people: but the Lord shall arise upon thee, and His glory shall be seen upon thee," (Isaiah 60:2).

Gideon's life *reflected* God's Glory.

Though he may have been "small," God's Glory was on his life. What you have within you will overshadow the gloom of the world around you.

"Thy word is a lamp unto my feet, and a light unto my path," (Psalm 119:105).

Though darkness may *cover* the earth, it will never rule over you because of The One to Whom you surrendered.

"Then spake Jesus again unto them, saying, I am the Light of the world: he that followeth Me shall not walk in darkness, but shall have the light of life," (John 8:12).

45

"As long as I am in the world, I am The Light of the world," (John 9:5).

A Word From the Lord Will Triumph Any Impending Circumstance.

Do not be disheartened because the prophecy spoken over your life *seems improbable.* Do not be dismayed because what you have been declaring and believing over your life *has not yet manifested.*

What? That Tiny Cloud!

A cloud the size of a man's hand was the *precursor* to a *deluge,* reversing a drought that had lingered for three years.

Elijah was not discouraged because the cloud never appeared *the first six times he prayed.* The rain still did not appear the *seventh* time he prayed either; *instead, a cloud the size of a man's hand* rose from the sea.

You would have thought that a *large* cloud would have been more appropriate. Yet, that cloud, though *small,* was the precursor to *a cloudburst.*

Elijah did not have to wait to *hear* raindrops to *know* there would be a thunderstorm. *That tiny cloud was evidence of the abundance of rain.*

"...and he cast himself down upon the earth, and put his face between his knees,

"And said to his servant, Go up now, look toward the sea. And he went up, and looked, and said, There is nothing. And he said, <u>Go again seven times</u>.

"And it came to pass at the seventh time, that he said, Behold,<u> there ariseth a little cloud out of the sea, like a man's hand</u>. And he said, Go up, say unto Ahab, Prepare thy chariot, and <u>get thee down, that the rain stop thee not</u>.

"And it came to pass in the mean while, <u>that the heaven was black with clouds and wind, and there was a great rain</u>," (1 Kings 18:42-45).

"A little one..." (Isaiah 60:22).

The Tiny Cloud You See Is Evidence of A Thunderstorm.

Do Not Be Discouraged Because You Are Starting Small.

"Shall Become..."
Isaiah 60:22

~ Secret #2 ~

Greatness Is A Process

"A little one **shall become...**" (Isaiah 60:22).

Where You Are Is Not Where You Will Stay.

Do not let your present circumstances talk you out of your dreams. Your current situation may be a *product* of your Past; however, your Present does not have the power to hold your Future *hostage* unless you let it.

Joseph received a picture of his Future. He saw himself in a position of *leadership...authority... influence...importance.* Yet, when he shared this with his brothers, they reacted with *hate*.

"And Joseph <u>dreamed a dream</u>, and he told it his brethren: and <u>they hated him yet the more</u>."

"For, behold, we were binding sheaves in the field, and, lo, my sheaf arose, and also stood upright; and, behold, <u>your sheaves stood round about, and made obeisance to my sheaf</u>.

"And he dreamed yet another dream, and told it his brethren, and said, Behold, I have dreamed a dream more; and, behold, <u>the sun and the moon and the eleven stars made obeisance to me</u>," (Genesis 37:5,7,9).

Your Dreams Will Provoke Reaction

Joseph's own father *rebuked* him when he shared the dream with him. He could not envision the *entire* family giving homage to Joseph. Yet, while Joseph's brothers *envied* him, his father spent time *contemplating* Joseph's words.

"And he told it to his father, and to his brethren: and <u>his father rebuked him</u>, and said unto him, What is this dream that thou hast dreamed? <u>Shall I and thy mother and thy brethren indeed come to bow down ourselves to thee to the earth</u>? And <u>his brethren envied him</u>; but his father observed the saying," (Genesis 37:10-11).

Envy, A Merciless Invader

Joseph's brothers' hatred intensified to the point they conspired to *kill* him. The feelings of hate became a conspiracy to commit *murder*. They even sarcastically referred to him as the dreamer.

"And when they saw him afar off, even before he came near unto them, they conspired against him to slay him.

"And they said one to another, Behold, this dreamer cometh.

"Come now therefore, and let us slay him, and cast him into some pit, and we will say, Some evil beast hath devoured him: and we shall see what will become of his dreams," (Genesis 37:18-20).

"Do Not Kill Him!"

Reuben, one of Joseph's brothers, *opposed* the plan to commit a homicide. He *intervened*. Reuben wanted to *preserve* Joseph's life by suggesting an *alternative*. He intended to *rescue* Joseph and *return him* to his father *alive*. The brothers agreed to cast him into a pit.

51

"And Reuben heard it, and he delivered him out of their hands; and said, <u>Let us not kill him</u>.

"And Reuben said unto them, Shed no blood, but <u>cast him into this pit</u> that is in the wilderness, and <u>lay no hand upon him</u>; that he might rid him out of their hands, <u>to deliver him to his father again</u>.

"And it came to pass, when Joseph was come unto his brethren, that they <u>stript Joseph out of his coat</u>, his coat of many colours that was on him;

"And they took him, and <u>cast him into a pit</u>: and the pit was empty, there was no water in it," (Genesis 37:21-24).

They *stripped* Joseph of his tunic, the coat of many colors. They took away what had been an integral part of his identity. Even before the dreams, Joseph had been singled out by his father as the *favorite*. The coat of many colors was an outward *expression* of his father's inward *feelings* toward him.

Hatred Grows

The Seed of Hatred was *first* sown when they discovered Joseph was his father's favorite, *and* everything else that happened after that amplified their open hostility toward him.

"Now Israel <u>loved Joseph more than all his children</u>, because he was the son of his old age: and he made him <u>a coat of many colours</u>.

"And when his brethren saw that their father loved him more than all his brethren, <u>they hated him, and could not speak peaceably unto him</u>," (Genesis 37:3-4).

Joseph sharing his dreams added fuel to the fire of hatred that *sparked* when his brothers perceived he was their father's *favorite* child.

The brothers were so *callous* toward Joseph that they could sit down and casually have a meal after putting him in the pit.

Feeding Hatred Schedules Disaster.

"Ye have heard that it was said by them of old time, Thou shalt not kill; and <u>whosoever shall kill shall be in danger of the judgment</u>:

"But I say unto you, That <u>whosoever is angry with his brother without a cause shall be in danger of the judgment</u>: and whosoever shall say to his brother, Raca, shall be in danger of the council: but whosoever shall say, Thou fool, shall be in danger of hell fire," (Matthew 5:21-22).

Sold As A Slave To Relatives

As his brothers shared the meal, they decided to turn their original plan into a *profitable* venture, so they sold him as a slave to some traveling merchants.

They *sold* their blood brother to distant relatives. The Ishmaelites were the descendants of Ishmael, the brother to their grandfather, Isaac.

"And they <u>sat down to eat bread</u>: and they lifted up their eyes and looked, and, <u>behold, a company of Ishmaelites</u> came from Gilead with their camels bearing spicery and balm and myrrh, going to carry it down to Egypt.

"And Judah said unto his brethren, <u>What profit is it if we slay our brother, and conceal his blood</u>?

"Come, and <u>let us sell him to the Ishmaelites</u>, and let not our hand be upon him; for he is our brother and our flesh. And his brethren were content," (Genesis 37:25-27).

Only after seeing the *possibility of profit*, did they recognize that he was their brother and their flesh. They *justified* selling him as a slave over killing him.

"Come, and let us sell him to the Ishmaelites, and <u>let not our hand be upon him; for he is our brother and our flesh</u>. And his brethren were content. Then there passed by Midianites merchantmen; and they drew and lifted up Joseph out of the pit, and sold Joseph to the Ishmaelites for twenty pieces of silver: and they brought Joseph into Egypt," (Genesis 37:27-28).

Family Secrets

The same argument Reuben used to convince his brothers to *preserve* Joseph's life was the same argument they used to *justify* the sale.

Joseph's brother, Reuben, returns to the pit to complete his *rescue* operation. He intends to *return* Joseph to his father in one piece before the brothers could have a change of heart and follow through with their premeditated murder plot.

Unbeknownst to Reuben, his brothers had already completed the transaction and handed over the merchandise. He finds an *empty* pit.

"And <u>Reuben returned unto the pit</u>; and, behold, <u>Joseph was not in the pit</u>; and he rent his clothes.

"And he returned unto his brethren, and said, <u>The child is not; and I, whither shall I go</u>?" (Genesis 37:25-30).

Misleading Evidence

Together, they stage evidence to *convince* their father that Joseph is no more. They let Jacob conclude that a wild animal had devoured Joseph.

"And they <u>took Joseph's coat</u>, and killed a kid of the goats, and <u>dipped the coat in the blood</u>;

"And they sent the coat of many colours, and they <u>brought it to their father</u>; and said, This have we found: know now whether it be thy son's coat or no.

"And he knew it, and said, <u>It is my son's coat; an evil beast hath devoured him</u>; Joseph is without doubt rent in pieces," (Genesis 37:31-33).

Imagine Joseph trying to reconcile the events of the past day or days. What started with him merely *obeying* his father's instruction has culminated in *slavery*. He went from being the *favorite* son, to being in a *pit,* to eventually being sold off in *captivity.* Whatever the form or fashion, this sequence of events did not resemble what Joseph witnessed in his dreams.

Your present circumstances will not always reflect that state of affairs you desire for your Future.

And The Lord Was With Joseph...

When Joseph was brought down to Egypt, someone in *leadership* and *authority* bought him off the Ishmaelites' hands. What is the *possibility* that Potiphar would be in that part of town conducting business at the same time Joseph is paraded in as a slave?

Notwithstanding his circumstances, The Lord was *ever present* in Joseph's life. "God is our Refuge and Strength, a very present Help in trouble," (Psalm 46:1).

The Bible repeatedly uses this phrase, "And The Lord was with Joseph..." When The Lord is with you, it does not matter what your Present looks like; *sooner or later, things will change.*

"And Joseph was brought down to Egypt; and Potiphar, an officer of Pharaoh, captain of the guard, an Egyptian, bought him of the hands of the Ishmaelites, which had brought him down thither.

"<u>And the Lord was with Joseph</u>, and he was <u>a prosperous man</u>; and he was in the house of his master the Egyptian.

"And <u>his master saw that the Lord was with him</u>, and that the Lord made all that he did to prosper in his hand.

"<u>And Joseph found grace in his sight</u>, and he served him: and <u>he made him overseer over his house, and all that he had he put into his hand.</u>

"And it came to pass from the time that he had made him overseer in his house, and over all that he had, that <u>the Lord blessed the Egyptian's house for Joseph's sake</u>; and the blessing of the Lord was upon all that he had in the house, and in the field," (Genesis 39:1-5).

In Captivity...Yet In Leadership

Joseph may have been a captive, nevertheless, he rose to a position of *authority*. The Bible described him as a *prosperous* man. How many slaves do you know that have been called prosperous? There are many people who, unlike Joseph, are living in *freedom*, yet they cannot be described as flourishing!

Potiphar, his master, recognized that The Lord was with him. Everything Joseph undertook was *successful*, so it pleased Potiphar to make him *overseer* over his whole house and everything he owned.

Potiphar *honored* the grace that was on Joseph's life, and in turn, the grace that was on Joseph's life brought great prosperity to Potiphar's household. Potiphar was *brilliant* in tapping into the anointing that was on Joseph's life.

What You Respect, You Draw Toward You.

What You Celebrate, Multiplies in Your Life.

"And he left all that he had in Joseph's hand; and he knew not ought he had, save the bread which he did eat. And Joseph was a goodly person, and well favoured," (Genesis 39:6).

59

During your journey in Greatness, you will encounter those who will be skillful in tapping into the grace that is on your life.

Hidden Distractions

Concealed along your journey in Greatness are traps. If satan cannot *stop* you from advancing in your Greatness, he will attempt to *sidetrack* you with something that *fragments* your focus or *compromises* your integrity.

Always Be Alert.

Never get too comfortable when you make it to the next level of your Greatness. Joseph recognized that any deviation from or compromise along his path in Greatness was tantamount to sinning against The Lord.

"And it came to pass after these things, that <u>his master's wife cast her eyes upon Joseph</u>; and she said, <u>Lie with me</u>.

"But <u>he refused</u>, and said unto his master's wife, Behold, my master wotteth not what is with me in the house, and he hath committed all that he hath to my hand;

"There is none greater in this house than I; neither hath he kept back any thing from me but thee, because thou art his wife: <u>how then can I do this great wickedness, and sin against God</u>?

"And it came to pass, as she spake to Joseph day by day, <u>that he hearkened not unto her</u>, to lie by her, or to be with her.

"And it came to pass about this time, that Joseph went into the house to do his business; and there was none of the men of the house there within.

And she caught him by his garment, saying, Lie with me: and <u>he left his garment in her hand, and fled</u>, and got him out," (Genesis 39:7-12).

Joseph Loses His Second Garment

Despite Potiphar's wife's *repeated* attempts to get Joseph to compromise, he remained *steadfast* in his resolve to honor God.

One day, she seductively seized his garment, probably thinking that he would not leave the room without it, but Joseph was willing to leave it behind so he could stay faithful to The Lord. Joseph did not abuse or overstep the favor he received by assuming he could partake of his master's wife!

Potiphar's wife took the garment and presented it to him as *evidence* to support her false accusation against Joseph's life. Since Joseph was a slave, everything that he had was given to him by Potiphar.

By presenting the garment to Potiphar, his wife essentially *accused* him of giving someone dangerous too much authority in their house. Since Potiphar made Joseph the overseer of his house and over all that he had, Joseph was probably his wife's boss; but he *refused* her invitation to become her lover too!

"And it came to pass, when she saw that <u>he had left his garment in her hand</u>, and was fled forth,

That she called unto the men of her house, and spake unto them, saying, See, <u>he hath brought in an Hebrew unto us to mock us</u>; he came in unto me to lie with me, and <u>I cried with a loud voice</u>:

"And it came to pass, when he heard that <u>I lifted up my voice and cried</u>, that he left his garment with me, and fled, and got him out.

"And she laid up his garment by her, until his lord came home.

"And she spake unto him according to these words, saying, <u>The Hebrew servant, which thou hast brought unto us, came in unto me to mock me</u>:

"And it came to pass, as <u>I lifted up my voice and cried, that he left his garment with me, and fled out.</u>

"And it came to pass, when his master heard the words of his wife, which she spake unto him, saying, After this manner did thy servant to me; that <u>his wrath was kindled</u>.

"And Joseph's master <u>took him, and put him into the prison</u>, a place where the king's prisoners were bound: and he was there in the prison," (Genesis 39:13-20).

A Tale of Two Garments

Joseph's first garment was the coat of many colors given to him by his father. It was a sign that he was the favorite...*an identity furnished on him by his father.*

Joseph was stripped of the garment, and the identity attached to it, when he was sold into slavery. *Who among his captors cared that he was the favorite son of Jacob?*

The second garment was left behind. It communicated his identity as the overseer of Potiphar's house and all his affairs. The garment represented...*an identity that was given to him by Potiphar.*

Joseph lost the garment and the identity attached to it, when he was falsely accused and thrown into prison. *Who in prison cared that he was the overseer of everything in Potiphar's household?*

One garment communicated Joseph's *death* to the one who conferred on him his first identity...*his father.* The other garment insinuated Joseph's *guilt* to the one who conferred on him his second identity... Potiphar.

Both garments were used to report in error.

Any Identity Man Gives You Can Be Compromised or Manipulated.

Your Real Identity

You Have a Real Identity.

Man cannot strip you of your real identity because man does not give it. Joseph saw *glimpses* of this identity in his dreams. The reaction he got when he shared those dreams is evidence his brothers only saw him according to the first identity that his father had conferred upon him...*the favorite child.*

Your Only Lasting Identity Is The One God Gives To You.

Focus on that identity instead of what your circumstances may be telling you.

Focus on where you are going, instead of what you are going through.

Focus on who you are, instead of what you are experiencing.

Your business may be *small* now, but that does not mean it will always be a small business. You may be holding an *entry-level* position where you work, but that does not mean that is where you will remain. You may have an idea for a business or a product, but no one seems interested in giving you the time of day. The *refusal* you face Today does not mean rejection is all you have to look forward to Tomorrow.

Your life *can* change.

Your life *will* change.

Look at where you are going instead of the circumstances around you.

What You Focus On You Eventually Replicate.

What You Look At The Longest Dominates Your Life.

What You Keep Looking At Is What You Eventually Become.

Prison Could Not Rob Joseph of His Identity

The Lord was still with Joseph.

Of all the prisons Potiphar could have sent Joseph, he was imprisoned where the king's prisoners were held.

Joseph may have lost two garments, *but he still had The Lord.* The Lord had mercy on Joseph and gave him Favor with the keeper of the prison. The keeper of the prison committed all the prisoners to Joseph's leadership.

"And Joseph's master took him, and put him into the prison, <u>a place where the king's prisoners were bound</u>: and he was there in the prison.

But <u>the Lord was with Joseph</u>, and shewed him mercy, and <u>gave him favour in the sight of the keeper of the prison.</u>

"And the <u>keeper of the prison committed to Joseph's hand all the prisoners that were in the prison;</u> and whatsoever they did there, he was the doer of it.

"The keeper of the prison looked not to any thing that was under his hand; because <u>the Lord was with him</u>, and that which he did, <u>the Lord made it to prosper</u>," (Genesis 39:20-23).

Joseph Had A Caring Heart

After Joseph's incarceration, two prominent offenders were imprisoned. They were both Pharaoh's officials. Of all the prisons they could have been sent to, they were dispatched to the same prison as Joseph. The captain of the guard put Joseph, a slave, in charge of two royal officials.

Divine Orchestration Does Not Always Look Like Divine Orchestration When It Occurs.

On a particular night, the two officials had dreams. When they awoke the next morning, they were both *visibly* shaken.

When Joseph walked up to them, he *noticed* they were both troubled. Their *depressed* mood got Joseph's *attention* because he had not seen them saddened or dismayed before.

Joseph was very *observant* and *compassionate*. He inquired of them what was causing them distress.

"And Joseph came in unto them in the morning, and <u>looked upon them, and, behold, they were sad</u>.

"And he asked Pharaoh's officers that were with him in the ward of his lord's house, saying, <u>Wherefore look ye so sadly to day</u>?" (Genesis 40:6-7).

Joseph Was Attentive To Those Under His Care

The two royal officials were *comfortable* enough to share their concerns with Joseph. He had developed a relationship with them such that they were *at ease* discussing their dreams with him. As officials who had served in the royal palace, they were probably very discreet or very measured in their conversations with others.

Yet, they were *willing* to open up to this Hebrew slave. Their concern was they did not know if they would ever deduce the meaning of their dreams. Little did they know, Joseph carried the *solution* to what was troubling them.

"And they said unto him, <u>We have dreamed a dream, and there is no interpreter of it</u>. And Joseph said unto them, <u>Do not interpretations belong to God? tell me them, I pray you</u>," (Genesis 40:8).

A Tale of Two Dreams

The chief butler was the *first* one to share his dream with Joseph. Joseph encouraged him that he would be *restored* to his former position with the king after three days. (See Genesis 40:9-13.)

Joseph then encouraged the chief butler to remember *him* when he got reinstated. He asked him to mention his case before Pharaoh. Joseph understood authority. He knew that one *higher* in command than the one who accused him could *reverse* his sentence. Joseph disclosed that he had been *unlawfully* brought to Egypt and was imprisoned based on a *false accusation.*

"But think on me when it shall be well with thee, and shew kindness, I pray thee, unto me, and make mention of me unto Pharaoh, and bring me out of this house:

"For indeed I was stolen away out of the land of the Hebrews: and here also have I done nothing that they should put me into the dungeon." (Genesis 40:14-15).

When the chief baker heard the interpretation, he also wanted to know what his dream meant. His dream did not have the same uplifting message as the other official. Within three days, he would be hung from a tree. (See Genesis 40:16-19).

Three days later, Pharaoh had a feast, and he did according to everything Joseph had spoken. The chief butler was *reinstated*, but the chief baker was *executed*.

"And <u>he restored the chief butler unto his butlership again</u>; and he gave the cup into Pharaoh's hand:

"But <u>he hanged the chief baker</u>: as Joseph had interpreted to them," (Genesis 40:21-22).

The Forgotten Deliverer

Even after the events unfolded exactly the way Joseph had laid out they would, the chief butler not only failed to remember to relay Joseph's message to Pharaoh; he forgot about him completely. It is understandable for something to slip someone's mind temporarily; however, it can be offensive if they *completely* forget!

"Yet did not the chief butler remember Joseph, but <u>forgat him</u>," (Genesis 40:23).

You can imagine how Joseph must have felt.

He encouraged the chief butler. He assisted him through a crisis. Yet, it took *two full years* before the chief butler *remembered* what he had done for him. (See Genesis 41:1,9-13).

"Until the time that his word came: <u>the word of the Lord tried him</u>," (Psalm 105:19).

You can imagine Joseph's *resolve* as he *anchored* his mind and thoughts on the dreams he had received as a child.

The Picture of Your Greatness Will Test You To See How Serious You Are For Its Fulfillment.

Crisis In The Palace

Two years after Joseph's encounter with the two royal officials, Pharaoh had two terrifying dreams. The next morning, he was so *troubled* that he called for all the magicians and wise men of Egypt to interpret the dream. *None of them could solve Pharaoh's predicament.*

"And it came to pass <u>at the end of two full years</u>, that <u>Pharaoh dreamed</u>: and, behold, he stood by the river.

"And it came to pass <u>in the morning that his spirit was troubled</u>; and he sent and <u>called for all the magicians of Egypt</u>, and <u>all the wise men</u> thereof: and Pharaoh told them his dream; but there was <u>none that could interpret them</u> unto Pharaoh," (Genesis 41:1,8).

The chief butler then remembered Joseph. As a butler, he was responsible for announcing those who wanted an audience with Pharaoh. As a chief butler, he was in a unique position to get people an audience with Pharaoh.

Yet, it took him two years to remember.

The chief butler told Pharaoh about what Joseph did for him. He did not even have to mention that Joseph had been brought to Egypt unlawfully. Nor did he say that Joseph had been falsely accused. The intensity of Pharaoh's pain trumped everything else.

Joseph's case got expedited.

"Then spake the chief butler unto Pharaoh, saying, <u>I do remember my faults this day</u>:

"Pharaoh was wroth with his servants, and put me in ward in the captain of the guard's house, both me and the chief baker:

"And we dreamed a dream in one night, I and he; we dreamed each man according to the interpretation of his dream.

"And <u>there was there with us a young man, an Hebrew, servant to the captain of the guard; and we told him, and he interpreted to us our dreams; to each man according to his dream he did interpret</u>.

"And it came to pass, <u>as he interpreted to us, so it was</u>; me he restored unto mine office, and him he hanged.

"Then <u>Pharaoh sent and called Joseph</u>, and they <u>brought him hastily out of the dungeon</u>: and he shaved himself, and changed his raiment, and came in unto Pharaoh," (Genesis 41:9-14).

A Crisis In The Palace Shone The Spotlight On The Prison.

You may be in a place in your life where it feels like you are in prison. A crisis in the palace will get Pharaoh to notice you. A dilemma in a position of authority will get those in leadership and those with influence to consult with you.

A Problem Is Looming Somewhere That Only You Are Qualified To Solve.

Just be diligent! "Seest thou <u>a man diligent</u> in his business? he <u>shall stand before kings</u>; he shall not stand before mean men," (Proverbs 22:29).

Those You Do Not Know... Will Come To Your Aid

Joseph did not know Pharaoh *personally*.

As Joseph sat in the pit, he did not know who Potiphar was. When Joseph was sent to prison, he did not think he would meet the baker.

Yet, it was foreigners who came to his aid. Those he did not grow up knowing. Those he probably least expected.

You may never know where your help will come from, but it will surely come...because of Whose you are.

"And the <u>Gentiles shall come to thy light</u>, and <u>kings to the brightness of thy rising</u>.

"Lift up thine eyes round about, and see: all <u>they gather themselves together, they come to thee</u>: thy sons shall come from far, and thy daughters shall be nursed at thy side.

"Then thou shalt see, and flow together, and thine heart shall fear, and be enlarged; because <u>the abundance of the sea shall be converted unto thee, the forces of the Gentiles shall come unto thee</u>. (Isaiah 60:3-5).

The *abundance* of the sea...shall be *yours*.

The *noise* of the sea...shall work in *your favor*.

The *forces* of wealth...shall flow *toward you*.

Remember Our Ultimate Example

Jesus was The Perfect Example of how to conduct yourself on your journey in Greatness.

"Looking unto Jesus the Author and Finisher of our faith; Who for the joy that was set before Him endured the cross, despising the shame, and is set down at the right hand of the throne of God," (Hebrews 12:2).

Have a *clear* picture of how you want your Greatness to look. Joseph *believed* in his dreams, which *affected* his future vision, which is why he was always *rising* to leadership positions wherever he was.

"And the Lord answered me, and said, <u>Write the vision, and make it plain upon tables, that he may run that readeth it</u>," (Habakkuk 2:2).

"For which of you, intending to build a tower, sitteth not down first, and <u>counteth the cost, whether he have sufficient to finish it</u>?" (Luke 14:28).

"<u>Where there is no vision, the people perish</u>: but he that keepeth the law, happy is he," (Proverbs 29:18).

Always remember, in the process of becoming, stay humble!

"Humble yourselves therefore under the mighty hand of God, <u>that He may exalt you</u> in due time," (1 Peter 5:6).

Jesus is our Ultimate Example.

"<u>Let this mind be in you, which was also in Christ Jesus</u>: Who, being in the form of God, thought it not robbery to be equal with God: But <u>made Himself of no reputation</u>, and <u>took upon Him the form of a servant</u>, and was <u>made in the likeness of men</u>: And being found in fashion as a man, <u>He humbled Himself</u>, and became obedient unto death, even the death of the cross. Wherefore <u>God also hath highly exalted Him</u>, and given Him <u>a Name which is above every name</u>," (Philippians 2:5-9).

You shall *ascend.*

You shall *mature.*

You shall *advance.*

You shall *transform.*

You shall *experience promotion.*

You shall *grow in influence.*

"A little one **shall become...**" (Isaiah 60:22).

Greatness Is A Process.

"A Thousand..."
Isaiah 60:22

~ Secret #3 ~

Greatness Is A Divine Achievement

"A little one shall become **a thousand...**" (Isaiah 60:22).

Greatness Is Your Divine Design.

When God first talked to Abraham, He spoke to him about Greatness. "Now the Lord had said unto Abram, Get thee out of thy country, and from thy kindred, and from thy father's house, unto a land that I will shew thee:

"And I will make of thee **a great nation**, and I will bless thee, and **make thy name great**; and thou shalt be a blessing;" (Genesis 12:1-2).

79

Greatness is on God's mind every time He talks to us. Your Greatness was on His mind *before* the foundation of the world.

Your Greatness matters to God.

"Blessed be the God and Father of our Lord Jesus Christ, <u>Who hath blessed us with all spiritual blessings in heavenly places in Christ</u>:

"<u>According as He hath chosen us in Him before the foundation of the world</u>, that we should be holy and without blame before Him in love:" (Ephesians 1:3-4).

"And hath raised us up together, and <u>made us sit together in heavenly places in Christ Jesus:</u>" (Ephesians 2:6).

The Goal of Every Divine Conversation

Every conversation God has with us is ultimately geared toward *leading* us to or *developing* us in our place of Greatness. It may be a word of *encouragement*...it may be *rebuke*...or it may even be a *warning*.

"And thine ears shall hear a word behind thee, saying, <u>This is the way, walk ye in it</u>, when ye turn to

8 Secrets To Remember On Your Journey In Greatness

the right hand, and when ye turn to the left," (Isaiah 30:21).

"Howbeit when He, the Spirit of truth, is come, <u>He will guide you into all truth</u>: for He shall not speak of Himself; but whatsoever He shall hear, that shall He speak: and <u>He will shew you things to come</u>," (John 16:13).

"The Lord will <u>perfect that which concerneth me</u>: Thy mercy, O Lord, endureth for ever: forsake not <u>the works of Thine own hands</u>," (Psalm 138:8).

"Being confident of this very thing, that <u>He Which hath begun a good work in you will perform it</u> until the day of Jesus Christ;" (Philippians 1:6).

"Shall I bring to the birth, and not cause to bring forth? saith the Lord: shall I cause to bring forth, and shut the womb? saith thy God," (Isaiah 66:9).

God Led Joseph In His Greatness

God was *actively* and *intimately* involved in Joseph's journey to and in Greatness.

"Until the time that his word came: <u>the word of the Lord tried him</u>," (Psalm 105:19).

"And <u>the Lord was with Joseph</u>, and he was a prosperous man; and he was in the house of his master the Egyptian," (Genesis 39:2).

"And <u>his master saw that the Lord was with him</u>, and that the Lord made all that he did to prosper in his hand," (Genesis 39:3).

"But <u>the Lord was with Joseph</u>, and shewed him mercy, and gave him favour in the sight of the keeper of the prison," (Genesis 39:21).

"The keeper of the prison looked not to any thing that was under his hand; because <u>the Lord was with him</u>, and that which he did, the Lord made it to prosper," (Genesis 39:23).

God led Pharaoh to ask for Joseph.

"And the <u>Gentiles shall come to thy light</u>, and <u>kings to the brightness of thy rising</u>," (Isaiah 60:3).

God created a crisis in the palace that *only* Joseph could solve. Pharaoh discovered that Joseph had a *solution* to his predicament, so he sent for him. Joseph was *hastily* brought before Pharaoh. (See Genesis 41:8-14.)

"Then <u>Pharaoh sent and called Joseph</u>, and they <u>brought him hastily out of the dungeon</u>: and he shaved himself, and <u>changed his raiment</u>, and came in unto Pharaoh," (Genesis 41:14).

Joseph *willingly* shaved and changed his garment. He was no longer a *hostage* to the identity that men gave him. Joseph no longer *tightly* held to an identity that had been given to him by another. He had *grown* into his Greatness.

This time, the garment was not forcibly taken from him; he freely released it. "He that findeth his life shall lose it: and he that loseth his life for my sake shall find it," (Matthew 10:39).

Joseph Stands Before Pharaoh

Every Arrival Is Simply A New Beginning.

Joseph acknowledged that the ability to interpret dreams came from The Lord. In so doing, he further acknowledged his identity was *connected* to The Lord and not to what people said of him. Pharaoh may have referred to him as one with the ability to understand and interpret dreams; however, Joseph *redirected* the focus on God.

"And Pharaoh said unto Joseph, I have dreamed a dream, and there is none that can interpret it: and <u>I</u>

have heard say of thee, that thou canst understand a dream to interpret it.

"And Joseph answered Pharaoh, saying, It is not in me: God shall give Pharaoh an answer of peace," (Genesis 41:15-16).

Even after Pharaoh shared his dream, Joseph reiterated that it was The Lord showing Pharaoh what was to come. He acknowledged the sovereignty of God...*even above Pharaoh.* "And Joseph said unto Pharaoh, The dream of Pharaoh is one: God hath shewed Pharaoh what He is about to do," (Genesis 41:25).

The Extra Mile

Joseph did not stop at the interpretation.

He recognized that Pharaoh had a looming crisis to resolve. The meaning of the dream was now evident in Pharaoh's eyes, but he did not have a plan to prepare for the seven years of *famine* that would follow the seven years of *abundance.*

Joseph was *proactive.*

Joseph demonstrated *initiative.*

Joseph presented Pharaoh with a *strategy* to prepare for the events that were about to unfold. He expressed *compassion* and *loyalty* to Pharaoh and the people of Egypt by alerting them that in following the plan their precious land will thrive in the famine and not perish.

Joseph also advised Pharaoh to *select* a man of impeccable and proven leadership ability to *oversee* the operation. He even proposed an administrative structure throughout the land of Egypt that would *facilitate* the execution of his plan.

A Unanimous Vote

All those in authority and leadership around Pharaoh *recognized* and *acknowledged* the brilliance of Joseph's plan.

There was no *dissident* voice. In Pharaoh's court, Joseph had no opposition.

He deciphered a problem none of them could solve. He proposed a strategy for the execution of a plan that would save their nation.

Joseph went from serving a wrongful prison sentence to solving a national crisis.

"Now therefore let Pharaoh look out <u>a man discreet and wise</u>, and <u>set him over the land of Egypt</u>.

"Let Pharaoh do this, and <u>let him appoint officers</u> over the land, and <u>take up the fifth part</u> of the land of Egypt <u>in the seven plenteous years</u>.

"And let them <u>gather all the food</u> of those good years that come, and lay up corn under the hand of Pharaoh, and let them <u>keep food in the cities</u>.

"And <u>that food shall be for store to the land against the seven years of famine</u>, which shall be in the land of Egypt; <u>that the land perish not</u> through the famine.

"And the thing was <u>good in the eyes of Pharaoh, and in the eyes of all his servants</u>," (Genesis 41:33-37).

Your Greatness May Be Muted, But It Cannot Be Silenced Forever.

A Promotion of Epic Proportions

Pharaoh then inquired among his servants if there was anyone with the *qualifications* to oversee such a *gargantuan* operation. Pharaoh *knew* that person would *need* to have the Spirit of God moving in their lives. He was aware that the dream was *from*

God, so whoever oversaw the plan's execution had to *have* God.

Joseph was the *obvious* choice.

He had *succeeded* where everyone had failed.

He had *thrived* where the very best in the land had floundered. *And it was widely known that The Lord was with him.*

"And Pharaoh said unto his servants, Can we find such a one as this is, <u>a man in whom the Spirit of God is</u>?

"And Pharaoh said unto Joseph, <u>Forasmuch as God hath shewed thee all this, there is none so discreet and wise as thou art</u>," (Genesis 41:38-39).

The Magnitude of The Problem You Solve Will Determine The Prominence of Your Promotion.

Pharaoh placed his *whole* house under the leadership of Joseph. Pharaoh promoted Joseph to the *highest* position in the land, second only to himself. What false accusation attempted to take away at Potiphar's house, God *restored* to Joseph at the *highest* government level.

Joseph became ruler over ALL the land.

Pharaoh took off his ring, an official symbol of authority, and placed it on Joseph's hand. Pharaoh dressed Joseph *differently*, but this time *the garments did not define him.*

Second In Command

Joseph rode around in a chariot just like Pharaoh did, with official runners *announcing* who he was and alerting people to bow. He received the *same* display of honor as if Pharaoh himself was riding around or entering a room.

Every person in Egypt was required to *submit* to his authority. Any event or any travel in the land was subject to Joseph's *authorization*.

"Thou shalt be over my house, and according unto thy word shall all my people be ruled: only in the throne will I be greater than thou.

"And Pharaoh said unto Joseph, See, I have set thee over all the land of Egypt.

"And Pharaoh took off his ring from his hand, and put it upon Joseph's hand, and arrayed him in vestures of fine linen, and put a gold chain about his neck;

"And he made him to <u>ride in the second chariot</u> which he had; and <u>they cried before him, Bow the knee</u>: and <u>he made him ruler over all the land of Egypt</u>.

"And Pharaoh said unto Joseph, I am Pharaoh, and <u>without thee shall no man lift up his hand or foot in all the land of Egypt</u>," (Genesis 41:40-44).

Instead of following an identity based on what a man had said, Joseph's identity was based on who God created him to be.

Heaven Is Involved In Your Greatness

Joseph's Greatness was *God-stamped.*

Joseph's Greatness was *God-approved.*

God approves of you becoming great.

God approves of you becoming *1,000 times more* than what you are now. Greatness is what He has *promised* through the Blessing of Abraham.

Receive it by grace through faith.

"The Lord God of your fathers <u>make you a thousand times so many more as ye are, and bless you, as He hath promised you!</u>" (Deuteronomy 1:11).

"And I will make of thee a great nation, and I will bless thee, and make thy name great; and thou shalt be a blessing:

"And I will bless them that bless thee (Abram), and curse him that curseth thee: and in thee shall all families of the earth be blessed," (Genesis 12:2-3).

"That the blessing of Abraham might come on the Gentiles through Jesus Christ; that we might receive the promise of the Spirit through faith," (Galatians 3:13-14).

"For by grace are ye saved through faith; and that not of yourselves: it is the gift of God," (Galatians 2:8).

Your Greatness Is God's Desire

God wishes you *prosper* even as your soul flourishes. As your mind, will and emotions thrive, so shall it be. Joseph's soul prospered, making it possible for him to engage at a higher and higher level.

Overseeing Pharaohs' affairs required a higher level of maturity and thinking than managing Potiphar's matters.

"Until the time that his word came: <u>the word of the Lord tried him</u>," (Psalm 105:19).

"Beloved, I wish above all things <u>that thou mayest prosper and be in health</u>, even <u>as thy soul prospereth</u>," (3 John 2).

"The multitude of camels <u>shall cover thee</u>, the dromedaries of Midian and Ephah; all they from Sheba shall come: <u>they shall bring gold and incense; and they shall shew forth the praises of the Lord.</u>

"All the flocks of Kedar <u>shall be gathered together unto thee</u>, the rams of Nebaioth <u>shall minister unto thee</u>: they shall come up with acceptance on Mine altar, and <u>I will glorify the house of My glory</u>," (Isaiah 60:6-7).

"A little one shall become **a thousand...**" (Isaiah 60:22).

You shall *lead*...1,000.

You shall *influence*...1,000.

You shall *become*...an army.

You shall *produce*...with the fruitfulness of a thousand.

The strength of one...shall become the power of 1,000. That army of 1,000 will in turn...lead 1,000 each.

That original little "one" will eventually lead 1,000,000.

Greatness Is A Divine Achievement.

Isaiah 60:22

"A little one...

    shall become...

        a thousand...

            and a small one...

                a strong nation:

                    I the Lord...

                        will hasten it...

                            in His time."

"A Small One..."
Isaiah 60:22

~ Secret #4 ~

Where You Are Now Is Not Where You Will Always Be

"A little one shall become a thousand, **and a small one...**," (Isaiah 60:22).

A Fruit Does Not Resemble The Seed.

An apple seed does not look like the *orchard* it carries. A zygote does not look like a fully-grown *adult*. Yet, the apple seed contains many orchards. The zygote contains the DNA of a fully-grown adult.

What appears at the *beginning* of a thing does not necessarily reflect how the *result* will look. Do not be discouraged by what you see at the beginning.

"Though thy beginning was small, yet thy latter end should greatly increase," (Job 8:7).

Do not be dismayed if everyone else seems to have advanced in life, and it appears that you have been left behind.

"So <u>the last shall be first</u>, and the first last: for many be called, but few chosen," (Matthew 20:16).

With God's hand on you, great things shall come out of your circumstances.

"And Nathanael said unto him, <u>Can there any good thing come out of Nazareth</u>? Philip saith unto him, Come and see," (John 1:46).

Yes, great things can come out of Nazareth!

"How <u>God anointed Jesus of Nazareth</u> with the Holy Ghost and with power: <u>Who went about doing good, and healing all that were oppressed of the devil</u>; for God was with Him," (Acts 10:38).

Are You Judging By The Manger...?

Anyone who would have judged Jesus by where He came from would have failed to see *where He was going* and *the impact His life would ultimately have* on all of humanity.

A manger does not look anything like a heavenly throne. What you see is inferior to what is in the unseen realm. The Presence of The Lord will *always* trump your natural circumstances.

"And she brought forth her firstborn Son, and wrapped Him in swaddling clothes, <u>and laid Him in a manger</u>; because there was no room for them in the inn.

"And there were in the same country shepherds abiding in the field, keeping watch over their flock by night.

"And, lo, <u>the angel of the Lord</u> came upon them, and <u>the glory of the Lord</u> shone round about them: and they were sore afraid.

"And the angel said unto them, Fear not: for, behold, I bring you good tidings of great joy, which shall be to all people.

"<u>For unto you is born this day in the city of David a Saviour, which is Christ the Lord.</u>

"And this shall be a sign unto you; Ye shall find the Babe wrapped in swaddling clothes, <u>lying in a manger</u>," (Luke 2:7-12).

Never judge your life's outcome by the "manger" you currently see or are presently living in.

Your Manger Is Not...Your Identity.

Your Manger Is Not...Your Future.

From The Manger To Heavenly Places

The manger did not define who Christ was and is. It was merely a point of entry into the earth...*it was only a starting point.*

"And what is the exceeding greatness of His power to us-ward who believe, according to the working of His mighty power,

"Which He wrought in Christ, when He raised Him from the dead, and <u>set Him at His own right hand in the heavenly places,</u>

"<u>Far above all</u> principality, and power, and might, and dominion, and every name that is named, not only in this world, but also in that which is to come:

"And hath put <u>all things under His feet</u>, and gave Him to be <u>the Head over all things</u> to the church,

"Which is His body, the fulness of Him that filleth all in all," (Ephesians 1:19-23).

Through what Christ did for us, we are seated *in heavenly places with Him.*

"But God, Who is rich in mercy, for His great love wherewith He loved us,

"Even when we were dead in sins, hath quickened us together with Christ, (by grace ye are saved;)

"And hath raised us up together, and made us sit together in heavenly places in Christ Jesus:

"That in the ages to come He might shew the exceeding riches of His grace in His kindness toward us through Christ Jesus," (Ephesians 2:4-7).

You Are Not A Hostage of Your Manger

Look to The Lord!

Just as Christ moved on from a manger and went on *to impact the whole of humanity,* you too can leave your "manger" and go on *to impact society.* Right now, where you are in life does not define who you will ultimately become or what you will eventually do. Do not let "small" circumstances dishearten you.

"The Lord maketh poor, and maketh rich: He bringeth low, and lifteth up.

"He <u>raiseth up the poor out of the dust</u>, and <u>lifteth up the beggar from the dunghill</u>, to <u>set them among princes</u>, and to <u>make them inherit the throne of glory</u>: for the pillars of the earth are the Lord's, and He hath set the world upon them," (1 Samuel 2:7-8).

The Unlikely Patriarch

Jacob grew up with the *stigma* of being a supplanter. At his birth, he emerged from the womb, *grabbing* the heel of his elder brother, Esau, and that was how he got his name.

"And after that came his brother out, and <u>his hand took hold on Esau's heel</u>; and <u>his name was called Jacob</u>: and Isaac was threescore years old when she bare them," (Genesis 25:26).

A *supplanter* is one who attempts to supersede, replace, or overthrow another.

Imagine living every waking breath of your life as someone perceived as a *schemer*, a *conniver*, one who *cannot be trusted*.

Imagine living as one always expected to do what is wrong or dishonorable.

That was the identity with which Jacob grew up.

That was the perception that defined his formative years. Isaac's estimation of Jacob persisted well into his old age. Esau's conception of his twin brother lingered well into their adult years. They both openly admitted to being a victim of it.

"And when Esau heard the words of his father, he cried with a great and exceeding bitter cry, and said unto his father, Bless me, even me also, O my father.

"And he said, <u>Thy brother came with subtilty</u>, and hath taken away thy blessing.

"And he said, Is not he rightly named Jacob? for <u>he hath supplanted me these two times</u>: he took away my birthright; and, behold, now he hath taken away my blessing. And he said, Hast thou not reserved a blessing for me?" (Genesis 27:34-36).

What they kept calling him is what eventually emerged. They ate "the fruit" of their words. (See Proverbs 18:21.)

God's Word Will Stand

Rebekah *struggled* to get pregnant.

She battled *barrenness*. Isaac prayed earnestly for her, and The Lord answered. He was a child of *promise* to Abraham. In turn, his children were also part of that promise that The Lord made to Abraham. It was The Lord's will for Isaac to have children.

"And Isaac was forty years old when he took Rebekah to wife, the daughter of Bethuel the Syrian of Paddan–aram, the sister to Laban the Syrian.

"And <u>Isaac entreated the Lord for his wife</u>, because <u>she was barren</u>: and the Lord was entreated of him, and <u>Rebekah his wife conceived</u>," (Genesis 25:20-21).

What Have You Been Praying For?

After conceiving, Rebekah developed a new prayer request. The babies jostled in her belly so much; she wondered why she had to go on living.

Sometimes, what we have been praying for gives us a different experience or outcome than what we had initially expected or anticipated.

Rebekah had to seek The Lord for answers.

"And the children struggled together within her; and she said, If it be so, why am I thus? And <u>she went to enquire of the Lord</u>.

"And the Lord said unto her, <u>Two nations are in thy womb</u>, and <u>two manner of people</u> shall be separated from thy bowels; and <u>the one people shall be stronger</u> than the other people; and <u>the elder shall serve the younger</u>," (Genesis 25:22-23).

Whatever Has Been Received Through Prayer Must Be Managed And Maintained With Prayer.

What God had told Rebekah about "the elder shall serve the younger" is what eventually happened. Jacob received the birthright and the blessing that ordinarily would have gone to Esau, the eldest child.

God's Word Overrules False Identity

The word of The Lord *stood* regardless of the scathing stigma and debilitating identity Jacob had endured while growing up.

"Therefore God give thee of the dew of heaven, and the fatness of the earth, and plenty of corn and wine:

"Let people serve thee, and nations bow down to thee: be lord over thy brethren, and let thy mother's sons bow down to thee: cursed be every one that curseth thee, and blessed be he that blesseth thee," (Genesis 27:28-29).

Later, Isaac sent Jacob to find a wife in the house of Bethuel, his mother's father. He did not want Jacob to take a wife from the daughters of Canaan.

Esau had, and Isaac was disappointed in him.

"And Isaac called Jacob, and blessed him, and charged him, and said unto him, Thou shalt not take a wife of the daughters of Canaan.

"Arise, go to Paddan–aram, to the house of Bethuel thy mother's father; and take thee a wife from thence of the daughters of Laban thy mother's brother," (Genesis 28:1-2).

Obedience Is A Qualifier

Jacob may have held a *supplanter's* identity, but he was a son who *obeyed* his parents' instructions. He was *qualified* to *provoke* and *attract* the Abrahamic blessing that Isaac still had to release, even after telling Esau he had no more blessing to impart.

"And God Almighty bless thee, and **make thee fruitful, and multiply thee, that thou mayest be a multitude of people**;

"<u>And give thee the blessing of Abraham, to thee, and to thy seed with thee</u>; that thou mayest inherit the land wherein thou art a stranger, which God gave unto Abraham.

"And Isaac sent away Jacob: and <u>he went to Paddan–aram unto Laban</u>, son of Bethuel the Syrian, the brother of Rebekah, Jacob's and Esau's mother.

"And that <u>Jacob obeyed his father and his mother</u>, and was gone to Paddan–aram;" (Genesis 28:3-5,7).

I am sure Isaac was *relieved* he had prayed the blessing over Jacob because of how *disappointed* he was with Esau. Esau was the poster child of what you should not do.

"When Esau saw that Isaac had blessed Jacob, and sent him away to Paddan–aram, to take him a wife from thence; and that as he blessed him <u>he gave him a charge, saying, Thou shalt not take a wife of the daughters of Canaan</u>;

"And Esau seeing that <u>the daughters of Canaan pleased not Isaac his father</u>;" (Genesis 28:6,8).

God's word over your life will stand.

Be Faithful In The Small Things

Jacob served Laban *faithfully.*

Be faithful wherever you are. "And if ye have <u>not been faithful</u> in that which is another man's, <u>who shall give you that which is your own</u>?" (Luke 16:12).

"A <u>faithful man shall abound with blessings</u>: but he that maketh haste to be rich shall not be innocent," (Proverbs 28:20).

He *endured* challenges, hardship, and deception for twenty years. Through it all, God was with him.

God brought him out.

"<u>This twenty years</u> have I been with thee; thy ewes and thy she goats have not cast their young, and the rams of thy flock <u>have I not eaten</u>.

"That which was torn of beasts I brought not unto thee; <u>I bare the loss of it</u>; <u>of my hand didst thou require it</u>, whether stolen by day, or stolen by night.

"Thus I was; in the day the drought consumed me, and the frost by night; and my sleep departed from mine eyes.

"Thus have I been twenty years in thy house; I served thee fourteen years for thy two daughters, and six years for thy cattle: and thou hast changed my wages ten times.

"Except the God of my father, the God of Abraham, and the fear of Isaac, had been with me, surely thou hadst sent me away now empty. God hath seen mine affliction and the labour of my hands, and rebuked thee yesternight," (Genesis 31:38-42).

You Can Finish Strong

Jacob started small but increased exceedingly.

"And **the man increased exceedingly**, and had much cattle, and maidservants, and menservants, and camels, and asses," (Genesis 30:43).

You are not alone.

You will receive...*help.*

You will receive...*resources.*

You will receive...*connections.*

The Lord will sustain you.

"Who are these that fly as a cloud, and as the doves to their windows?

"Surely the isles shall wait for Me, and the ships of Tarshish first, <u>to bring thy sons from far, their silver and their gold with them</u>, unto the name of the Lord thy God, and to the Holy One of Israel, <u>because He hath glorified thee</u>," (Isaiah 60:8-9).

You have Great Value

You *carry* the promise of something great.

You *house* the Seed of your Future and the Future of so many others. Just like Laban sought Jacob and ended up making amends with him, those that oppressed or afflicted you when you were *small*... when you were *little*...when you were *insignificant*... when your *idea did not make sense*...when your *plan sounded unreasonable*...when your *strategy seemed to fail*...when your *thoughts carried no weight*...shall come back to show you Honor.

"The sons also of <u>them that afflicted thee shall come bending unto thee</u>; and <u>all they that despised thee shall bow themselves down at the soles of thy feet</u>; and they shall call thee, The city of the Lord, The Zion of the Holy One of Israel.

"Whereas thou hast been forsaken and hated, so that no man went through thee, <u>I will make thee an eternal excellency, a joy of many generations</u>. (Isaiah 60:14-15).

The Seemingly Insignificant Beginnings In Your Own Life...Can Create A Tsunami of Blessing In The Lives of So Many Others.

"The hands of Zerubbabel <u>have laid the foundation of this house; his hands shall also finish it;</u> and thou shalt know that the Lord of hosts hath sent me unto you.

"**For who hath despised the day of small things?** for <u>they shall rejoice</u>, and shall see the plummet in the hand of Zerubbabel with those seven; they are the eyes of the Lord, which run to and fro through the whole earth," (Zechariah 4:9-10).

Where You Are Now Is Not Where You Will Always Be.

"*A Strong Nation...*"
Isaiah 60:22

~ Secret #5 ~
Your Journey Will Birth
A Movement

"A little one shall become a thousand, and a small one **a strong nation...**" (Isaiah 60:22).

Sorrow Can Birth Passion.

When Nehemiah *heard* about the conditions of the Jews who had survived in exile and the wreckage of Jerusalem's walls, he was left with a *heavy* heart. He was so *moved* by what he heard that he *fasted* and *prayed* before The Lord.

"And they said unto me, The remnant that are left of the captivity there in the province <u>are in great affliction and reproach</u>: the <u>wall of Jerusalem also is broken down</u>, and the <u>gates thereof are burned with fire</u>.

"And it came to pass, when I heard these words, that <u>I sat down and wept</u>, and <u>mourned certain days, and fasted</u>, and <u>prayed before the God of heaven</u>," (Nehemiah 1:3-4).

Nehemiah *interceded* for the children of Israel. He humbly confessed any sins they may have committed, including his own. Nehemiah *accepted* the responsibility to make things right. He took *ownership* of what had happened. Nehemiah *resolved* to intercede both day and night. He did not try to accuse or apportion blame to others.

Taking Personal Responsibility

When You Apportion Blame To Others, You Deprive Yourself of The Ability To Make Any Meaningful Changes.

Nehemiah acknowledged the *faithfulness* of God and the *unfaithfulness* of the children of Israel. He recognized they were where they were as a nation because of what they had done as a nation.

"And said, <u>I beseech thee</u>, O Lord God of heaven, the Great and Terrible God, <u>that keepeth covenant and mercy</u> for them that love Him and observe His commandments:

"Let Thine ear now be attentive, and Thine eyes open, that Thou mayest hear the prayer of Thy servant, <u>which I pray before thee now, day and night</u>, for the children of Israel Thy servants, and <u>confess the sins of the children of Israel, which we have sinned against Thee: both I and my father's house have sinned.</u>

"<u>We have dealt very corruptly against Thee</u>, and have not kept the commandments, nor the statutes, nor the judgments, which Thou commandedst Thy servant Moses," (Nehemiah 1:5-7).

Nehemiah knew that the children of Israel were reaping the *consequences* of their actions. He also learned about a *promise* The Lord had made to Moses.

Remind The Lord of His Promises

The Lord had also made way for the children of Israel to be *restored* unto Him. He promised to *re-establish* them if they *returned* to Him and *purposed* to walk in obedience. Nehemiah *reminded* The Lord of the commitment He had made to Moses and the children of Israel.

"Remember, I beseech Thee, the word that Thou commandedst Thy servant Moses, saying, If ye transgress, I will scatter you abroad among the nations:

"But if ye turn unto Me, and keep My commandments, and do them; though there were of you cast out unto the uttermost part of the heaven, yet will I gather them from thence, and will bring them unto the place that I have chosen to set My name there," (Nehemiah 1:8-9).

In the scriptures, The Lord *repeatedly* invites us to approach Him.

"Put Me in remembrance: let us plead together: declare thou, that thou mayest be justified," (Isaiah 43:26).

"Thus saith the Lord, the Holy One of Israel, and his Maker, Ask Me of things to come concerning My sons, and concerning the work of My hands command ye Me," (Isaiah 45:11).

Boldly Approach The Lord

As a child of God, you can *boldly* approach Him to *remind* Him of the promises spoken over your life.

You have a High Priest, The Lord Jesus Christ, who *feels* what you are feeling.

"For we have not an High Priest Which cannot be touched with the feeling of our infirmities; but <u>was in all points tempted like as we are, yet without sin.</u> Let us therefore <u>come boldly unto the throne of grace, that we may obtain mercy, and find grace</u> to help in time of need," (Hebrews 4:15-16).

Besides, The Lord even promises The Holy Spirit, not only to *teach* you, but to help you *remember* what you have been taught, what you have been *promised,* and what you are *entitled* to as His child.

"But the Comforter, *which* is the Holy Ghost, Whom the Father will send in My name, <u>He shall teach you all things, and bring all things to your remembrance, whatsoever I have said unto you,</u>" (John 14:26).

Help Is Available

Deeply affected by the plight of his people, Nehemiah decided to discuss it with the king. He served in the king's court as a cupbearer. One can only imagine how many issues Nehemiah may have thought of to discuss with the king because of the access he had to him, but did not because they were either too trivial or not worthy of the king's attention.

However, this was one that he could not ignore.

Nehemiah needed The Lord to favor his conversation with the king. The wellbeing of God's people was at stake.

What he felt on the inside had to be voiced.

"Now these are Thy servants and Thy people, whom Thou hast redeemed by Thy great power, and by Thy strong hand.

"O Lord, I beseech Thee, let now Thine ear be attentive to the prayer of Thy servant, and to the prayer of Thy servants, who desire to fear Thy name: and prosper, I pray thee, Thy servant this day, and grant him mercy in the sight of this man. For I was the king's cupbearer," (Nehemiah 1:10-11).

When Nehemiah stood next in the presence of the king, he offered him wine. Nehemiah did not *initiate* the conversation.

He simply served.

"And it came to pass in the month Nisan, in the twentieth year of Artaxerxes the king, that wine was before him: and <u>I took up the wine, and gave it unto the king</u>. Now <u>I had not been beforetime sad in his presence</u>.

"Wherefore the king said unto me, <u>Why is thy countenance sad, seeing thou art not sick? this is nothing else but sorrow of heart</u>. Then I was very sore afraid," (Nehemiah 2:1-2).

Royal Expectations

Serving in the king's court was considered a *privilege*, especially for an exile. You can imagine the standard of excellence that was *required* when operating in the palace.

Joy.

Cheerfulness.

Anything less might be perceived as *unhappiness* or *discontentment* with your position, or *ungratefulness* with the opportunity you have been given. A glum look on the face of an exile could be interpreted as the desire or preference to be in their home country rather than where they are serving.

117

In a king's mind, "What better place to serve is there than in my court? Why would anybody want to work anywhere else?"

The *penalty* for a bad attitude in the palace was probably *severe*. Remember the butler and the baker who shared prison quarters with Joseph? (See Genesis 40.)

The *happiness* of the servant is something that matters in the king's court. It is a *reflection* of the king. Even the Queen of Sheba noticed the countenance of those that served in King Solomon's court. (See 1 Kings 10:8.)

Nehemiah's Work Ethic

Nehemiah had made an *impression* on King Artaxerxes. Think it not a light thing for an exile to be serving him wine. Of all the positions that would require extreme vetting, this would be one of them.

King Artaxerxes was very *perceptive*. Nehemiah did not have a history of a sad countenance in his presence, so his facial expression stood out. The king knew Nehemiah was not sick. He knew Nehemiah was dealing with a matter of the heart.

"Wherefore the king said unto me, Why is thy countenance sad, seeing thou art not sick? <u>this is nothing else but sorrow of heart</u>. Then I was very sore afraid," (Nehemiah 2:2).

Nehemiah *freely* and *openly* shared with the king what was troubling him. He did not attempt to *disassociate* himself from who his people were and the conditions they faced.

"And said unto the king, Let the king live for ever: <u>why should not my countenance be sad,</u> when the city, the place of my fathers' sepulchres, <u>lieth waste, and the gates thereof are consumed with fire</u>?" (Nehemiah 2:3).

Your Opportunity Will Come

King Artaxerxes could have responded by asking Nehemiah why he was so concerned about his people, yet he had the privilege of serving in the land's highest office. He could have accused Nehemiah of disloyalty toward his kingdom in expressing grief over the children of Israel.

Instead, King Artaxerxes asked Nehemiah what he *needed*. He wanted to be a *solution* to what was causing grief in the heart of his servant. Nehemiah, sensing this to be the God-opportunity he had been praying for, consulted with The Lord.

"Then the king said unto me, For what dost thou make request? So I prayed to the God of heaven," (Nehemiah 2:4).

Nehemiah was *swift* to tell the king he wanted to be involved in *rebuilding* the city. He asked the king to consider his track record and history with the king as a factor in making his decision. You can only make such a claim if you have been an *exceptional* worker where you currently serve.

"And I said unto the king, If it please the king, and if thy servant have found favour in thy sight, that thou wouldest send me unto Judah, unto the city of my fathers' sepulchres, that I may build it," (Nehemiah 2:5).

King Artaxerxes' *only question* was, "How long will it take?" That was all he was concerned about as he made a favorable decision. The king *wanted* Nehemiah to *return* to him when he was done.

"And the king said unto me, (the queen also sitting by him,) For how long shall thy journey be? and when wilt thou return? So it pleased the king to send me; and I set him a time," (Nehemiah 2:6).

You Will Have Access To Resources

Nations are not built in a day.

Nehemiah did not initially *lead* the children of Israel, but he was *given authority by the one who ruled **a strong nation***. Nehemiah did not initially *govern* Israel either, but he had at his disposal *the resources of the one who commanded **a strong nation***.

"Moreover I said unto the king, If it please the king, <u>let letters be given me</u> to the governors beyond the river, <u>that they may convey me over</u> till I come into Judah;

"And <u>a letter unto Asaph</u> the keeper of the king's forest, <u>that he may give me timber</u> to make beams for the gates of the palace which appertained to the house, and for the wall of the city, and for the house that I shall enter into. <u>And the king granted me, according to the good hand of my God upon me</u>.

"Then I came to the governors beyond the river, and gave them the king's letters. <u>Now the king had sent captains of the army and horsemen with me</u>," (Nehemiah 2:7-9).

Never Give Up On Your Vision

Nehemiah had the king's *authority*, the king's *endorsement*, and the king's *resources*, working in his favor, according to the hand of The Lord upon his life.

"And <u>the sons of strangers shall build up thy walls, and their kings shall minister unto thee</u>: for in My wrath I smote thee, but <u>in My favour have I had mercy on thee</u>," (Isaiah 60:10).

Nehemiah envisioned a restored city.

"Therefore thy gates shall be open continually; they shall not be shut day nor night; <u>that men may bring unto thee the forces of the Gentiles, and that their kings may be brought</u>," (Isaiah 60:11).

You, too, have the hand of The Lord upon your life to bring to pass the things which The Lord has promised you, *no matter how unlikely that outcome may look at the moment.*

You may not have *all* the resources you want and need right now, but rest assured you are *connected* to The One Who *owns* everything.

Hold Fast To The Vision of Your Future.

Your Vision Will Attract Attention

One of the most potent forces on the earth is...*vision with momentum.*

Do Not Let Your Vision "Stop" With You.

Your vision has the potential...*to bless many others.* Your dream has the potential...*to be embraced by others.* Your dream has the potential...*to be perpetuated by others.*

A man may be "killed," but death will not necessarily "contain" his vision. If his vision has been received and embraced by others, it will be perpetuated. A dead man who left a vision is better than a living man without one. A man without a vision is as loud as *the whisper of his coffin.*

Let Your Vision Spread!

"And the Lord answered me, and said, Write the vision, and make it plain upon tables, that he may run that readeth it," (Habakkuk 2:2).

"Where there is no vision, the people perish," (Proverbs 29:18).

The rulers among the children of Israel saw Nehemiah's *commitment.* They knew who he was and the resources available to him. They knew he had purposed to *rebuild* Jerusalem. They could see his *determination,* to see Jerusalem no longer the subject of ridicule or the source of shame. Most of all, they knew *the hand of The Lord* was upon him.

"And the rulers knew not whither I went, or what I did; neither had I as yet told it to the Jews, nor to the priests, nor to the nobles, nor to the rulers, nor to the rest that did the work.

"Then said I unto them, <u>Ye see the distress that we are in</u>, how Jerusalem lieth waste, and the gates thereof are burned with fire: <u>come, and let us build up the wall of Jerusalem, that we be no more a reproach</u>.

"Then I told them of <u>the hand of my God which was good upon me</u>; as also the king's words that he had spoken unto me. And they said, Let us rise up and build. So they strengthened their hands for this good work," (Nehemiah 2:16-18).

Building On The Right Foundation

As Nehemiah expounded on the resources he had at his disposal, he started by telling them about how *the hand of The Lord* was upon his life.

That was the first thing he emphasized.

"Then I told them of <u>the hand of my God which was good upon me</u>; as also the king's words that he had spoken unto me," (Nehemiah 2:18a).

He wanted to communicate the *importance* of the hand of The Lord on their efforts, over anything else they should access. Only after talking about the hand of The Lord did he share with them the king's words.

Nehemiah knew God was their Source.

Nehemiah knew this was The Lord's doing.

"But <u>if ye turn unto Me</u>, and keep My commandments, and do them; though there were of you cast out unto the uttermost part of the heaven, yet <u>will I gather them from thence, and will bring them unto the place that I have chosen to set My name there</u>," (Nehemiah 1:9).

Nehemiah *built* the vision on *the right Foundation*; the hand of The Lord, not the king's words.

"Then I told them of <u>the hand of my God which was good upon me</u>; as also the king's words that he had spoken unto me," (Nehemiah 2:18a).

Vision Becomes A Movement

After Nehemiah established the vision on the right Foundation and shared about the resources they had access to, the people were *inspired* to participate. They all knew the part they had to play.

They *caught* the vision.

They *embraced* the vision.

They *resolved* to run with the vision.

Their participation became a movement.

"Then I told them of the hand of my God which was good upon me; as also the king's words that he had spoken unto me. <u>And they said, Let us rise up and build. So they strengthened their hands for this good work</u>," (Nehemiah 2:18).

"And the Lord answered me, and said, Write the vision, and make it plain upon tables, <u>that he may run that readeth it</u>," (Habakkuk 2:2).

Your Movement Will Inspire Opposition

Nehemiah's vision was to *restore* Jerusalem, a symbol of identity and pride to the children of Israel. Sanballat and Tobiah were severely *upset* that someone would care about their welfare. They were happier with Jerusalem in a state of *shame*.

"When Sanballat the Horonite, and Tobiah the servant, the Ammonite, <u>heard of it, it grieved them exceedingly that there was come a man to seek the welfare of the children of Israel</u>," (Nehemiah 2:10).

When they saw that Nehemiah was doing something about Israel's welfare, they stepped up their *opposition*. They launched a political agenda *alleging* Nehemiah was rebelling against the king; little did they know he was acting with the king's blessing.

"But when Sanballat the Horonite, and Tobiah the servant, the Ammonite, and Geshem the Arabian, heard it, <u>they laughed us to scorn, and despised us, and said, What is this thing that ye do? will ye rebel against the king?</u>" (Nehemiah 2:19).

Remember Your Foundation

Nehemiah did not respond to Sanballat and Tobiah by telling them that he had letters from the king. Instead, he *stood* on his Foundation.

The Foundation on which he had built the vision. The Foundation that was *superior* to any authority that the king could give. Nehemiah kept his focus on *The God of Heaven.*

"Then answered I them, and said unto them, <u>The God of heaven, He will prosper us; therefore we His servants will arise and build</u>:" (Nehemiah 2:20).

Nehemiah *reminded* them that they had no stake, no claim, or history to Jerusalem. Since they had no part in it, their opinions were of no consequence.

"...but ye have <u>no portion, nor right, nor memorial</u>, in Jerusalem," (Nehemiah 2:20).

Despite their repeated efforts to *sabotage* the rebuilding of Jerusalem's walls and gates, Sanballat and Tobiah *failed*.

Relentlessly Resist Distractions

Broken Focus Is The Recipe For Failure.

Jesus is The Perfect Example of how to *stay focused* on the Divine Task God has given you.

"Looking unto Jesus the Author and Finisher of our faith; Who <u>for the joy that was set before Him endured the cross, despising the shame,</u> and is set down at the right hand of the throne of God," (Hebrews 12:2).

Nehemiah *refused* to be sidetracked.

He *declined* Sanballat's invitation to meet in the plain of Ono. Behind his outward show of hospitality, Sanballat was *concealing* an evil plan...*a stumbling block*. Nehemiah's focus kept him from *entrapment*.

"Now it came to pass when Sanballat, and Tobiah, and Geshem the Arabian, and the rest of our enemies, heard that I had builded the wall, and that there was no breach left therein; (though at that time I had not set up the doors upon the gates;)

"That Sanballat and Geshem sent unto me, saying, <u>Come, let us meet together</u> in some one of the villages in the plain of Ono. But <u>they thought to do me mischief</u>, (Nehemiah 6:1-2).

Nehemiah's *preoccupation* with his Divine Assignment kept him from danger. Your *laser focus* on what God has called you to do will keep you from becoming a *hostage* to the agenda of your enemy.

Nehemiah was unwilling to *sacrifice* his work to *satisfy* the request of someone who had *openly* shown his opposition to what he was called to do. Do not surrender your Divine Assignment to the *whims* of critics.

"And I sent messengers unto them, saying, <u>I am doing a great work</u>, so that I cannot come down: <u>why should the work cease</u>, whilst I leave it, and come down to you?" (Nehemiah 6:3).

Become Comfortable Saying, "No!"

Let people become *accustomed* to your "No!"

Do not be moved by their *persistence*. Your Assignment is too precious to be *compromised*.

"Yet they <u>sent unto me four times</u> after this sort; and <u>I answered them after the same manner</u>.

"Then sent Sanballat his servant unto me in like manner <u>the fifth time</u> with an open letter in his hand;" (Nehemiah 6:4-5).

When Sanballat realized that his tactics were not working, he decided to *change* his approach. He *falsely accused* Nehemiah of having an *ulterior* motive. Interesting, he was the one with the *covert* agenda. Sanballat accused Nehemiah of coveting a leadership position, yet that is what was clearly on *his* mind. Why would Sanballat be *unsettled* at the reestablishment of Jerusalem?

Sanballat even attempted to *mask* his allegations by attributing the accusatory statements to the *neighboring* nations, then purported to act in an advisory capacity since news of this would be sent to the king.

False Accusation Reveals Intent

Sometimes, your enemy's intent is revealed in their accusations.

False Accusation Thrives On The Lips of Those Who Are Threatened By You.

"Wherein was written, It is <u>reported among the heathen</u>, and Gashmu saith it, that <u>thou and the Jews think to rebel</u>: for which cause thou buildest the wall, <u>that thou mayest be their king</u>, according to these words.

"And thou hast also appointed prophets to preach of thee at Jerusalem, saying, There is a king in Judah: and <u>now shall it be reported to the king</u> according to these words. Come now therefore, and <u>let us take counsel together</u>," (Nehemiah 6:6-7).

Defy False Accusation

Do not take the bait.

False accusation is designed to *rob* you of productivity. False accusation is designed to *remove* your focus from your Assignment. False accusation is designed to *channel* your energy and resources *away* from what God has called you to do.

Nehemiah was *unmoved* by the claim that the false reports will reach the king. "...and <u>now shall it be reported to the king</u> according to these words," (Nehemiah 6:7).

Nehemiah knew well *the Foundation* he was standing on and what God had called him to do. He knew the accusation had been *fabricated*.

"Then I sent unto him, saying, <u>There are no such things done as thou sayest</u>, but <u>thou feignest them out of thine own heart</u>," (Nehemiah 6:8).

Look To God For Strength

Instead of allowing his attention to be held hostage by the allegations, he *focused* on The Foundation. He discerned that the charges were intended to amplify *weakness* and spread *fear* among them.

Nehemiah focused on God for strength!

"For <u>they all made us afraid, saying, Their hands shall be weakened</u> from the work, that it be not done. Now therefore, O God, <u>strengthen my hands</u>," (Nehemiah 6:9).

As you face the false accusation, do not try to resist it on your own. Look to The Lord for strength.

Let Him order your steps through it all.

When Sanballat and Tobiah realized that all their methods for derailing the work had not worked, they attempted a "spiritual" approach. They recognized how *devoted* Nehemiah was to The Lord, so they *fashioned* a plan of attack using what he held most dear. They contracted a priest to give him a *false* prophecy; a prophecy cloaked as *protection* from his enemies.

"Afterward I came unto the house of Shemaiah the son of Delaiah the son of Mehetabeel, who was shut up; and he said, <u>Let us meet together in the house of God</u>, within the temple, and let us shut the doors of the temple: for they will come to slay thee; yea, <u>in the night will they come to slay thee</u>," (Nehemiah 6:10).

Your Focus Will Expose Error

Nehemiah had *confidence* and was *fully persuaded* in what he was called to do. Anything that would harbor *fear* or attempt to *take him away* from completing the task was not from God.

Having asked God for *strength* to do the work God had called him to do, why would God now tell him to *hide*? (See Nehemiah 6:9.)

Nehemiah knew his Assignment was to complete the work, *not save himself.*

Protection was God's concern, not his!

Nehemiah discerned that Shemaiah was not acting in truth. His enemies had *hired* him with a goal to steer him off course, and thereby *cause* him to *sin.*

"And I said, <u>Should such a man as I flee</u>? and who is there, that, being as I am, would <u>go into the temple to save his life</u>? I will not go in.

"And, lo, <u>I perceived that God had not sent him</u>; but that he pronounced this prophecy against me: <u>*for Tobiah and Sanballat had hired him*</u>," (Nehemiah 6:11-12).

Your Focus Will Preserve Your Reputation

Shemaiah's goal was to *stain* Nehemiah's reputation, thereby *undermining* his credibility among those that stood with him. The plan was to push Nehemiah to *act in fear* and, therefore, *in sin, behaving contrary to God's will.*

How could those who stood with Nehemiah follow someone who was preoccupied with protecting himself and not them?

The false accusation that Nehemiah wanted to be king would have been fueled by him trying to preserve his own life instead of staying focused on rebuilding Jerusalem.

Self-preservation would have been perceived as *an act of fear,* an act which would have displayed a *lack of confidence* in God and His ability to preserve them as they continued in this great work.

"Therefore was he hired, <u>that I should be afraid, and do so, and sin,</u> and <u>that they might have matter</u>

for an evil report, that they might reproach
me," (Nehemiah 6:13).

God Will "Reward" Your Enemies

Nehemiah prayed that Sanballat and Tobiah
would be judged for all the mischief they had done.

"My God, think Thou upon Tobiah and
Sanballat according to these their works, and on the
prophetess Noadiah, and the rest of the prophets,
that would have put me in fear," (Nehemiah 6:14).

God promises to come against those who
sabotage, plot against, and frustrate His children.

"And I will bless them that bless thee, and curse
him that curseth thee: and in thee shall all families of
the earth be blessed," (Genesis 12:3).

"But thus saith the Lord, Even the captives of
the mighty shall be taken away, and the prey of the
terrible shall be delivered: for I will contend with him
that contendeth with thee, and I will save thy
children," (Isaiah 49:25).

"For the nation and kingdom that will not serve
thee shall perish; yea, those nations shall be utterly
wasted," (Isaiah 60:12).

Sanballat and Tobiah's plan failed.

"So <u>the wall was finished</u> in the twenty and fifth day of the month Elul, in fifty and two days. (Nehemiah 6:15)

"And it came to pass, that <u>when all our enemies heard thereof, and all the heathen that were about us saw these things, they were much cast down in their own eyes</u>:" (Nehemiah 6:16).

Nehemiah identified The God of Heaven as *The Foundation of his vision.* (See Nehemiah 2:20.)

If Nehemiah had referenced *the king* as the foundation of his vision, the work would have been *a hostage* to any political agenda that Sanballat and Tobiah could fabricate in the ears of the king during his lifetime or in the lifetime of those that reigned after him. (See Ezra 4.)

Sanballat and Tobiah *acknowledged* that they were no match for the hand of God. They recognized they were no match for Who Nehemiah had established as The Foundation of his vision.

"...for <u>they perceived that this work was wrought of our God</u>," (Nehemiah 6:16).

"For the nation and kingdom <u>that will not serve thee shall perish; yea, those nations shall be utterly wasted</u>," (Isaiah 60:12).

Nehemiah was successful.

Nehemiah completed the task.

"So <u>the wall was finished</u>..." (Nehemiah 6:15)

"The glory of Lebanon shall come unto thee, the fir tree, the pine tree, and the box together, <u>to beautify the place of My sanctuary; and I will make the place of My feet glorious</u>," (Isaiah 60:13).

You Will Finish "Your Wall"

You will be successful.

You will complete the task.

There was a celebration in Jerusalem.

"And Nehemiah, which is the Tirshatha, and Ezra the priest the scribe, and the Levites that taught the people, said unto all the people, <u>This day is holy unto the Lord your God; mourn not, nor weep.</u> For all the people wept, when they heard the words of the law.

"Then he said unto them, Go your way, eat the fat, and drink the sweet, and send portions unto them for whom nothing is prepared: for <u>this day is holy unto our Lord: neither be ye sorry; for the joy of the Lord is your strength</u>," (Nehemiah 8:9-10).

The joy of The Lord is your strength.

You will *celebrate.* You will not mourn, for your victory is *holy* unto The Lord.

You will birth...*a strong lifestyle.*

You will birth...*a vibrant nation.*

You will birth...*an influential culture.*

You will birth...*an impactful mindset.*

You will birth...*a notable organization.*

Your Journey Will Birth A Movement.

"*I The Lord...*"
Isaiah 60:22

~ Secret #6 ~
God Will Introduce Himself

"A little one shall become a thousand, and a small one a strong nation: **I the Lord...**" (Isaiah 60:22).

The Lord Is With You.

"Let your conversation be without covetousness; and be content with such things as ye have: for He hath said, <u>I will never leave thee, nor forsake thee</u>," (Hebrews 13:5).

Do You Understand The Credentials of The One Who Said He Would Never Leave You Nor Forsake You?

141

The 4-Fold Promise

God made the promise to Jacob.

God assured Jacob, *He will keep him wherever he went.*

"And, behold, I am with thee, and <u>will keep thee in all places whither thou goest</u>, and will bring thee again into this land; <u>for I will not leave thee, until I have done that which I have spoken to thee of</u>," (Genesis 28:15).

God made the same promise to Israel. It is a promise that *imparts strength, courage and drives away fear.*

"Be strong and of a good courage, <u>fear not, nor be afraid of them</u>: for the Lord thy God, <u>He it is that doth go with thee; He will not fail thee, nor forsake thee</u>.

"And the Lord, <u>He it is that doth go before thee; He will be with thee, He will not fail thee, neither forsake thee: fear not, neither be dismayed</u>," (Deuteronomy 31:6,8).

God made the same promise to Joshua. It is a promise that *guarantees relentless victories.*

"<u>There shall not any man be able to stand before thee all the days of thy life</u>: as I was with Moses, so I will be with thee: <u>I will not fail thee, nor forsake thee</u>," (Joshua 1:5).

God made the same promise to Solomon. It is a promise *you will complete your Kingdom call.*

"And David said to Solomon his son, Be strong and of good courage, and do it: fear not, nor be dismayed: for the Lord God, even my God, will be with thee; <u>He will not fail thee, nor forsake thee, until thou hast finished all the work for the service of the house of the Lord</u>," (1 Chronicles 28:20).

May God keep you wherever you go.

May you receive strength and courage, and may all fear leave you.

May you walk in relentless victories.

May you complete your Kingdom call.

As Jesus ascended into Heaven, He echoed the same commitment to the disciples as they went forth and did His work.

"<u>Go ye therefore</u>, and teach all nations, baptizing them in the name of the Father, and of the Son, and of the Holy Ghost: Teaching them to observe all things whatsoever I have commanded you: and, lo, <u>I am with you alway, even unto the end of the world. Amen</u>," (Matthew 28:19-20).

Is God Qualified?

When a man makes a promise to you, the fulfillment of that vow is predicated on their *ability*, their *mood*, their *resources*, their *connections*, and their *limitations*.

What happens when their capabilities are *hampered?* What happens when their mood *changes?* What happens when they *no longer have* the contacts they thought they had? What happens when delivering on the commitment they initially made to you ends up being *beyond* their ability?

Has the fulfillment of their obligation to you now become a hostage to what they currently have no control over or what they can no longer influence?

The Lord is no *captive* to what hinders men.

"Behold, I am the Lord, the God of all flesh: <u>is there any thing too hard for Me</u>?" (Jeremiah 32:27).

"<u>God is not a man</u>, that He should lie; neither the son of man, that He should repent: hath He said, and shall He not do it? or hath He spoken, and shall He not make it good?" (Numbers 23:19).

"And He said, The things which are <u>impossible with men are possible with God</u>," (Luke 18:27).

Look To The Lord

Years ago, a man of God said to me, "Paul, if you seek favor with one man, that favor can be jeopardized when that one person has a mood swing, receives a false report about your life, or you disagree. However, if you look to The Lord and let Him favor your life, the day will never come when you lack Favor. If a person God has been using to show you favor decides to change, God can always raise another. When you look to The Lord, you will never be a prisoner to the favor of one person. God uses many channels."

"Being confident of this very thing, <u>that He which hath begun a good work in you will perform it until the day of Jesus Christ:</u>" (Philippians 1:6).

I have a cousin who *always* reads this next couple of verses every time he *share*s scripture. A *snippet* of scripture, yet it carries a *veritable* message, one that warrants reading *repeatedly*.

"I will lift up mine eyes unto the hills, from whence cometh my help. <u>My help cometh from the Lord, which made heaven and earth</u>," (Psalm 121:1-2).

The Lord made heaven and earth.

What problem under the sun could you possibly face that He would be *unable* to solve?

"Behold, <u>the Lord's hand is not shortened</u>, that it cannot save; neither His ear heavy, that it cannot hear:" (Isaiah 59:1).

"Now <u>unto Him that is able</u> to do exceeding abundantly above all that we ask or think, according to the power that worketh in us," (Ephesians 3:20).

Do You Feel Like You Are On The Run?

Seemingly overnight, Jacob became like a *fugitive*. He had *impersonated* his brother, Esau, and received the father's blessing in his stead.

Now, here he was *running* for his life.

So much for the blessing, huh?

His brother, Esau, hatched a plan to *kill* him. Rebekah, his mother, was alerted about his brother's intentions. She approached Isaac to save Jacob.

146

Rather than mentioning Esau's intentions, she told Isaac she was concerned about Jacob *marrying* the same kind of woman Esau had married. She knew Isaac was *not pleased* with the prospect of his sons marrying Canaanite women. So, Isaac instructed Jacob to *leave* home and *look* for a wife at his mother's brother's house. (See Genesis 27-28.)

Here we have Jacob with all this weighing on his heart. He had to *depart* from his home, a place that he had known all his life, and forge his way into the *unknown*.

Maybe you are feeling the same way!

Take some time to *refresh* yourself.

Take some time to *rejuvenate* yourself.

Take some time to *sit alone* with The Lord.

How Has God Visited You Lately?

The Lord appeared to Jacob during the calm amid his crisis.

"And Jacob went out from Beer–sheba, and went toward Haran.

147

"And he lighted upon a certain place, and tarried there all night, because the sun was set; and he took of the stones of that place, and put them for his pillows, and lay down in that place to sleep.

"And he dreamed, and behold a ladder set up on the earth, and the top of it reached to heaven: and behold the angels of God ascending and descending on it.

"And, behold, the Lord stood above it, and said, I am the Lord God of Abraham thy father, and the God of Isaac: the land whereon thou liest, to thee will I give it, and to thy seed;" (Genesis 28:10-13).

God will *reveal* Himself in ways *through* your journey that He will never reveal anywhere else.

God *introduced* Himself to Jacob.

God presented Himself as a *Covenant Keeper.*

God Addressed Jacob's Future

God blessed Jacob with *territory.*

God blessed Jacob with *posterity.*

God showed up *loaded with promises.*

God talked to him first about the *land*, then about *his family* that will occupy the land. He spoke of *provision*, then about *posterity*. As in The Garden of Eden, God started with everything else and then gave man the family to put in it.

"And, behold, the Lord stood above it, and said, I am the Lord God of Abraham thy father, and the God of Isaac: <u>the land whereon thou liest, to thee will I give it, and to thy seed</u>;

"And **thy seed shall be as the dust of the earth**, and **thou shalt spread abroad** to the west, and to the east, and to the north, and to the south: and **in thee and in thy seed shall all the families of the earth be blessed**," (Genesis 28:13-14).

This scripture is reminiscent of Isaiah 60:22; the theme of this book... "A little one shall become a thousand, and a small one a strong nation: **I the Lord...**" (Isaiah 60:22).

God blessed Jacob with *His Presence, Protection, Guidance,* and promise of *Restoration.*

"And, behold, <u>I am with thee</u>, and <u>will keep thee in all places whither thou goest</u>, and <u>will bring thee again into this land</u>; for I will not leave thee, until I have done that which I have spoken to thee of," (Genesis 28:15).

Jacob Recognized God's Visitation

When Jacob woke up, he knew something *supernatural* had happened. This was not a dream he was going to forget. This was an encounter worth *recognizing* and *celebrating*.

Jacob was aware of his connection to God.

"And Jacob awaked out of his sleep, and he said, <u>Surely the Lord is in this place</u>; and I knew it not.

"And he was afraid, and said, <u>How dreadful is this place!</u> this is none other but the house of God, and <u>this is the gate of heaven</u>," (Genesis 28:16-17).

Consider again the credentials of The One Who said He would never leave you or forsake you.

God is in *Covenant* with you.

God is *committed* to your success.

When God raises you, your success is a *reflection* of Him. Your success reflects the hand of God in your life. Your success *showcases* His Power. Your success *proves* His Covenant. Your success *unveils* His Kingdom. When God calls, *endorses*, and *validates* you, He will make you succeed *for His Name's sake.*

"The Lord is my Shepherd; I shall not want.

"He maketh me to lie down in green pastures: He leadeth me beside the still waters.

"He restoreth my soul: He leadeth me in the paths of righteousness <u>for His Name's sake</u>," (Psalms 23:1-3).

A Trial Is Not A Failure.

A trial is simply an opportunity to *validate* your success. There is no failure when God is involved.

I challenge you to think of anything God is genuinely involved with that is wallowing in failure?!

So long as you keep holding fast to God, you will never be a failure.

Jacob Celebrated His Divine Encounter

Jacob took the time to *celebrate* and *commemorate* what The Lord had done in his life. He renamed the place of his encounter, God's House (Bethel). The place was initially called Luz, but Jacob renamed it Bethel. He was passionate enough about the location of his encounter to rename it and confer upon it an entirely different identity.

"And Jacob rose up early in the morning, and took the stone that he had put for his pillows, and set it up for a pillar, and <u>poured oil upon the top of it</u>.

"And <u>he called the name of that place Beth–el</u>: but the name of that city was called Luz at the first," (Genesis 28:18-19).

Jacob Was Moved To Make A Vow

The Divine Visitation *intensified* Jacob's walk and *commitment* to God. Jacob made a *covenant* with The Covenant Keeper. If God would provide His Presence, Protection, Guidance, Provision, and ultimately grant him Restoration to his father's house, he would give God a *tenth* of everything He blessed him.

"And <u>Jacob vowed a vow</u>, saying, If God will <u>be with me</u>, and will <u>keep me</u> in this <u>way that I go</u>, and will give me <u>bread to eat, and raiment to put on</u>,

"So that I <u>come again to my father's house in peace</u>; then shall the Lord be my God:

"And this stone, which I have set for a pillar, shall be God's house: and <u>of all that Thou shalt give me I will surely give the tenth unto Thee</u>," (Genesis 28:20-22).

When God's hand is on something, that is His *endorsement*...His personal *commitment;* He upholds His Covenant with His *excellent standard of righteousness.*

"Fear thou not; for I am with thee: be not dismayed; for I am thy God: I will strengthen thee; yea, I will help thee; yea, <u>I will uphold thee with the right hand of My righteousness</u>," (Isaiah 41:10).

Jacob Faces His Greatest Fear

Jacob served Laban, Rebekah's brother, for *twenty* years; *fourteen* years for his two daughters and *six* years for the cattle. During that time, Laban *changed* his wages ten times. When Laban and Jacob eventually parted ways, they made a covenant and left each other in peace. (See Genesis 31.)

After leaving Laban's house, Jacob dealt with the *stress* of a reunion with Esau. He recalled Esau's plan to *kill* him. Jacob now had wives, children, servants, and livestock.

Would Esau slaughter them all?

God was faithful to His Covenant with Jacob.

Even before Jacob met Esau, God dispatched angels to *meet* him. Nevertheless, Jacob was still greatly *distressed* when his messengers told him about those in Esau's company.

"And Jacob went on his way, and <u>the angels of God met him</u>. And when Jacob saw them, he said, <u>This is God's host</u>: and he called the name of that place Mahanaim," (Genesis 32:1-2).

"And the messengers returned to Jacob, saying, We came to thy brother Esau, and also he cometh to meet thee, and four hundred men with him.

"Then <u>Jacob was greatly afraid and distressed</u>..." (Genesis 32:6-7).

Jacob Reminds God of His Promise

Jacob cried out to The Lord for help. Jacob recognized that the blessing of family and possessions that he had received was from The Lord. Jacob crossed Jordan very differently than twenty years prior. He *reminded* The Lord of His Covenant of Protection, Preservation, and Restoration.

"And Jacob said, O God of my father Abraham, and God of my father Isaac, <u>the Lord Which saidst</u>

unto me, Return unto thy country, and to thy kindred, and I will deal well with thee:

"I am not worthy of the least of all the mercies, and of all the truth, which Thou hast shewed unto Thy servant; for with my staff I passed over this Jordan; and **now I am become two bands**.

"Deliver me, I pray thee, from the hand of my brother, from the hand of Esau: for I fear him, lest he will come and smite me, and the mother with the children.

"And Thou saidst, **I will surely do thee good, and make thy seed as the sand of the sea, which cannot be numbered for multitude**," (Genesis 32:9-12).

That night, after Jacob gave his company instructions to cross the brook, he spent some time in solitude. The events that would transpire the next day probably weighing *heavily* on his heart. (See Genesis 32.)

Jacob Wrestles Till Daybreak

Jacob ends up *wrestling* a Man until daybreak. Jacob wrestling this Man *physically* draws a parallel to how he was wrestling with his fears *internally*.

"And Jacob was left alone; <u>and there wrestled a Man with him until the breaking of the day</u>," (Genesis 32:24).

When the Man realized that He could not *defeat* Jacob, He threw Jacob's hip out of joint.

"And when He saw that He prevailed not against him, <u>He touched the hollow of his thigh; and the hollow of Jacob's thigh was out of joint</u>, as he wrestled with Him," (Genesis 32:25).

Even after the hip injury, Jacob *refused* to let Him go. He *insisted* on receiving a blessing as the condition for release. Jacob recognized there was something Divine about the Man he wrestled.

"And He said, Let Me go, for the day breaketh. And he said, <u>I will not let Thee go, except Thou bless me</u>.

"And He said unto him, What is thy name? And he said, Jacob.

"And He said, <u>Thy name shall be called no more Jacob, but Israel: for as a prince hast thou power with God and with men, and hast prevailed</u>," (Genesis 32:26-28).

"...a small one **a strong nation**..." (Isaiah 60:22).

How was Jacob able to prevail?

Through the power of Covenant.

Imagine wrestling your greatest fear, only to discover it was The Lord, conferring upon you your *new* identity!

Jacob Received A New Identity

Jacob received a new name. *Israel.*

For the *first* time in his life, how he saw himself *changed*. He now had the *God-perspective.* He now saw himself as someone who has a *voice* with God and with men. A *winner* and not a loser.

Society could no longer brand Jacob as a *supplanter*. He did not live at the *mercy* of others. He was no longer a *captive* to Laban. He was no longer *fearful* and on the run from Esau.

He was living his covenant rights.

That angelic encounter and identity change *shaped* his reunion with Esau. He approached Esau *confidently* as his own man. God also gave him *favor* with Esau. Esau was *happy* to see him. The assassination plot was long forgotten.

Jacob, now Israel, gave Esau a gift, even when Esau resisted receiving it from him. Esau eventually obliged. Jacob did not accept having Esau's men assigned to his camp, and *cordially* held his ground. He let Esau know he would manage without them. Esau *peacefully* honored Jacob's sentiments. (See Genesis 33.)

"A little one shall become a thousand, and a small one a strong nation: **I the Lord...**" (Isaiah 60:22).

Take A Step of Faith

Consider again the credentials of The One Who said He would never leave you nor forsake you.

The Lord of lords...

The King of kings...

The Mighty One of Jacob...

Our Provider...

Our Healer...

Our Protector...

Our Deliverer...

Our Strength...

Our Fortress...

Our Strong Tower...

Our Teacher...

Our Redeemer...

Make a more substantial commitment to Him. He is worthy of the best that we have to give.

"Thou shalt also suck the milk of the Gentiles, and shalt suck the breast of kings: and thou shalt know that <u>I the Lord am thy Saviour and thy Redeemer, the Mighty One of Jacob</u>.

"For brass <u>I will bring gold</u>, and for iron <u>I will bring silver</u>, and for wood <u>brass</u>, and for stones <u>iron</u>: I will also make <u>thy officers peace</u>, and <u>thine exactors righteousness</u>.

"<u>Violence shall no more be heard in thy land</u>, wasting nor destruction within thy borders; but <u>thou shalt call thy walls Salvation, and thy gates Praise</u>.

"<u>Thy people also shall be all righteous</u>: they <u>shall inherit the land for ever</u>, the branch of My planting, the work of My hands, that I may be glorified," (Isaiah 60:16-18,21).

You will prevail through The Covenant.

God Will Introduce Himself.

Isaiah 60:22

"A little one...

shall become...

a thousand...

and a small one...

a strong nation:

I the Lord...

will hasten it...

in His time."

"Will Hasten It..."
Isaiah 60:22

~ Secret #7 ~
God's Definition of Speed

"A little one shall become a thousand, and a small one a strong nation: I the Lord **will hasten it...**" (Isaiah 60:22).

God Has A Different Definition of Speed.

"For <u>My thoughts are not your thoughts, neither are your ways My ways</u>, saith the Lord.

"For as the <u>heavens are higher than the earth</u>, so are My ways higher than your ways, and My thoughts than your thoughts," (Isaiah 55:8-9).

God *created* time, but He exists *outside* of time. The *natural* world is framed by *time*, but the *spiritual* world exists *outside* of time constraints. The natural world operates *within* the boundaries of a *finite* schedule...*time*. The spiritual world works in the realm of an *infinite* timeline...*eternity*.

You are a spiritual being *housed* in a natural body. While you are housed in your *natural* body, you are referred to as a *human being*. When you *leave* your natural body, you will still exist as a *spiritual being*.

You are a spiritual being who *will live into eternity*. The question is, will you spend eternity *with The Lord*, or will you spend it *without* Him? Will you spend eternity in *everlasting fellowship* with Our Creator, Our Lord, and Savior, or will you spend it in *never-ending separation* from Him, in infinite severance from Love, Joy, and Peace.

That is a choice you must make.

"And as it is appointed unto men <u>once to die</u>, but <u>after this the judgment</u>:

"So <u>Christ was once offered to bear the sins of many</u>; and unto them that look for Him shall He appear the second time <u>without sin unto salvation</u>," (Hebrews 9:27-28).

"For God so loved the world, that He gave his only begotten Son, that <u>whosoever believeth in Him should not perish, but have everlasting life</u>," (John 3:16).

Do Not Be Discouraged By Scoffers

The enemy will contest any word or promise from God that you have received. The devil *reacts* to whatever is a threat or will be a threat to him and his agenda. You must stay *mindful* and *attentive* to the Divine words and promises that have been pronounced over your life.

"...I stir up your pure minds by way of remembrance: <u>That ye may be mindful</u> of the words which were spoken before by the holy prophets, and of the commandment of us the apostles of the Lord and Saviour:" (2 Peters 3:1-2).

Many have scoffed at the Return of Christ.

Scoffers do not focus on the power of the *promise* but their *agenda*. Scoffers are preoccupied with what they can *criticize*, instead of what they can *build* and where they can breathe *life*.

Scoffers *fuel* their criticism with what they can *see* in the natural. They *refuse* to see beyond their natural point of view because they are *preoccupied* with their carnal desires.

"Knowing this first, that <u>there shall come in the last days scoffers</u>, walking after their own lusts,

"And saying, <u>Where is the promise</u> of his coming? for since the fathers fell asleep, all <u>things continue as they were from the beginning</u> of the creation," (2 Peters 3:3-4).

God's Promises To You

Never *waver* in your expectation.

Grow in your *knowledge* of Him.

"According as His divine power <u>hath given unto us all things that pertain unto life and godliness, through the knowledge of Him</u> that hath called us to glory and virtue:

"Whereby <u>are given unto us exceeding great and precious promises</u>: that by these ye might be <u>partakers of the divine nature</u>, having escaped the corruption that is in the world through lust. (2 Peter 1:3-4).

God's Word is *preserving* your promise, regardless of your circumstances. God's Word is not subject to your circumstances. *Your experiences are subject to God's Word.*

The same Word that *created* the heavens and the earth is the same Word that is *speaking on your behalf.* That same Word is *preserving* you and your promise.

"But the heavens and the <u>earth, which are now, by the same word are kept in store</u>, reserved unto fire against the day of judgment and perdition of ungodly men," (2 Peter 3:7).

Speak God's Word

Keep *declaring* God's Word over your life.

Keep *speaking* God's Word over what you believe will happen. Keep God's Word *on your lips.*

"Thou shalt also <u>decree a thing</u>, and it shall be established unto thee: and the light shall shine upon thy ways," (Job 22:28).

"Let the <u>words of my mouth</u>, and the meditation of my heart, be acceptable in Thy sight, O Lord, my Strength, and my Redeemer," (Psalm 19:14).

"Death and life are in <u>the power of the tongue</u>: and they that love it shall eat the fruit thereof," (Proverbs 18:21).

When you say what God says, your words will not return to you void. Your words will *produce* fruit.

"So shall My word be that goeth forth out of My mouth: it <u>shall not return unto Me void</u>, but it <u>shall accomplish</u> that which I please, and it <u>shall prosper</u> in the thing whereto I sent it," (Isaiah 55:11).

Expect Divine Acceleration

Just because you may not have experienced *divine acceleration* before, do not *assume* that it cannot happen to you.

The man at the pool of Bethesda had not experienced *Divine* Healing before. He had spent almost 40 years trying to get his healing, but other people would beat him to it; yet he *persisted*. (See John 5:2-5).

How *discouraging*.

How *unfortunate*.

The fact that he had not experienced healing before did not *disqualify* him from the reality that Jesus was going to heal him. The Bible paints a picture that there was a great multitude of sick people there.

"In these lay a <u>great multitude of impotent folk</u>, of blind, halt, withered, waiting for the moving of the water," (John 5:3).

If many have said they have not received the promises they have been believing God for, that does not mean you have to *accept* that as your portion. Of all the people that were waiting for their healing beside the pool of Bethesda, how interesting is it that *Jesus singled this man out*?

"When <u>Jesus saw him lie</u>, and <u>knew that he had been now a long time in that case</u>, He saith unto him, Wilt thou be made whole?" (John 5:6).

He Almost Missed It

Jesus invited him to a *change* in the status quo.

Jesus asked him if he would like to *receive* his Divine Acceleration. Jesus never inquired *why* he had not been healed. Jesus did not ask him for a *list* of his challenges. Jesus did not ask him how *long* he had been sick.

"When Jesus saw him lie, and knew that he had been now a long time in that case, He saith unto him, <u>Wilt thou be made whole</u>?" (John 5:6).

Jesus was asking him if he wanted to *experience* Divine Acceleration at that moment.

"The impotent man answered him, Sir, I have no man, when the water is troubled, to put me into the pool: but while I am coming, another steppeth down before me.

"Jesus saith unto him, <u>Rise, take up thy bed, and walk.</u>

"And <u>immediately the man was made whole, and took up his bed, and walked</u>: and on the same day was the sabbath," (John 5:7-9).

Peter Wanted Us To Remember This

Of all the things the Apostle Peter shared in 2 Peter 3, the *one* thing that he *emphasized* for us to never be *unaware* of is, time does not constrain God. God can *transcend* time.

"But, beloved, <u>be not ignorant of this one thing</u>, that one day is with the Lord as a thousand years, and a thousand years as one day," (2 Peter 3:8).

God can do in one day what takes man 1,000 years to do. God can turn out the productivity of 1,000 years in one day.

Many may quote this scripture as a *pacifier* for a delay. On the contrary, this scripture references that no matter how long you have been waiting, *you can receive it today!*

This scripture is not to be used as an attempt to explain why something has not happened, or as a way to justify unproductive, helpless waiting. Instead, this is *militant advocacy* for the fact that your miracle, promise, or deliverance, can happen at any time.

Think about the man who *attempted* to get into the pool for 38 years, but *failed*. Did he know how *close* he was to his healing 5 minutes before it happened? How about 2 minutes before?

You may never know how *close* you are to your miracle; however, the time of your blessing is NOW!

Peter Even Gave Proof

It is evident that The Apostle Peter did not mean that a day with The Lord is as a thousand years and a thousand years as is a day with The Lord, to *justify* a delay in the manifestation of what we believe God to do in our lives.

Look at what he writes *immediately* afterward.

"The Lord is not slack concerning His promise, as some men count slackness; but is longsuffering to us-ward, not willing that any should perish, but that all should come to repentance," (2 Peter 3:9).

God is not *slow* or *lethargic*. Neither is He *negligent* when it comes to His promises. God takes *ownership* of the promises He makes. God is not an absentee father who makes commitments he cannot honor. He is not a shady businessman who writes checks that cannot be cashed!

To say that you must wait 1,000 years for something that takes one day is to label The Lord as the master of procrastination.

Have you ever dropped off an application at a government office, only to be told that it will be processed in a few weeks when in reality, the actual handling time could be 30 minutes? How did that make you feel? *Loved* or disappointed?

Double-Portion Delay

Does it make sense for our Savior to allow Himself to be *nailed* to The Cross for us, declare it is *finished, die,* and then *rise* on the third day, only to say to you, "Beloved, I need you to wait 1,000 more years!"

Technically more than 1,000 years have passed since The Resurrection of our Lord and Savior, so, if someone was going to argue in favor of delay, *over 2,000 years have passed since The Cross*. If they wanted to advocate "double-portion delay" (2,000 years), more than enough time has already passed! (Smile)

Take note of this one thing; God is no slacker.

"But, beloved, be not ignorant of this one thing...The Lord is not slack concerning His promise...," (2 Peter 3:8-9).

Rename Your Delays

Now that we have established delays are not because of God's inability or slowness, let's examine what the scripture says.

"The Lord is not slack concerning His promise, as some men count slackness; but is <u>longsuffering to us-ward, not willing that any should perish, but that all should come to repentance</u>," (2 Peter 3:9).

Any "delay" in your circumstance is for the benefit of *adding* more souls into The Kingdom and for your *preservation* when you eventually receive it.

"And account that <u>the longsuffering of our Lord is salvation</u>; even as our beloved brother Paul also according to the wisdom given unto him hath written unto you;" (2 Peter 3:15).

A Blessing Received Before The Recipient Is Mature Enough To Handle It Is No Longer A Blessing.

Whatever you have believed for and however long it has taken, just know...*it can happen today.* Your blessing can arrive "as a thief in the night...," (2 Peter 3:10).

When you have no picture on your flat-screen TV, do you blame the cable company or turn on the power?

Live a lifestyle that reflects your *expectation* of the manifestation of your *blessing*...what you are be*lieving* from God.

Your waiting season should *enhance* your level of *right living* before The Lord. Stay *plugged in* to The Source. Stay in *obedience*.

"...what manner of persons <u>ought ye to be in all holy conversation and godliness,</u>

"<u>Looking for and hasting</u> unto the coming of the day of God...

"Nevertheless we, according to His promise, look for new heavens and a new earth, <u>wherein dwelleth righteousness.</u>

"Wherefore, beloved, seeing that ye look for such things, <u>be diligent</u> that ye may be found of Him <u>in peace, without spot, and blameless</u>," (2 Peter 3:11-14).

Walk Diligently Before The Lord

Live your life *committed* to The Lord.

Do not be *sluggish*. Do not be *casual* about your *relationship* with The Lord. Do not be *lazy* in your *communion* with Him. He is not *slack* concerning His promises to you, so do not be *slothful* in your commitment to Him.

Be diligent.

Remain *resolute* in your *faith*.

Remain *persistent* in your *patience*.

Learn from those who, through faith and patience, *received* their promises from The Lord. In this book, you read about Abraham, Gideon, Joseph, Jacob, and their journey to obtain their promises. You, too, are on your path to *inherit* your promises.

You, Too, Are On Your Journey In Greatness.

"That ye <u>be not slothful</u>, but followers of them who through faith and patience inherit the promises," (Hebrews 6:12).

Authorization At The Highest Level

No authority *greater* than God has ever existed, can exist, or will ever exist! None superior to Him could ever *ratify* and *validate* His promise to Abraham, so He took it upon Himself to *authenticate* the covenant with His character and reputation, *a rock-solid guarantee.*

Abraham's promise received the *highest* and *greatest* seal of approval. The manifestation of it remained *inevitable*, even before any evidence existed.

"For when God made promise to Abraham, <u>because He could swear by no greater, He sware by Himself,</u>

"Saying, Surely blessing I will bless thee, and multiplying I will multiply thee," (Hebrews 6:13-14).

Knowing that manifestation was inevitable, all Abraham had to do was *patiently* endure regardless of the circumstances. His journey in Greatness was paved with *persevering endurance*.

"And so, after he had <u>patiently endured</u>, he <u>obtained the promise</u>," (Hebrews 6:15).

The Contractual Process

The *validity* and *strength* of a covenant are determined by the *authority* that *enforces* it. That is why men sign contracts in business. A contract spells out each party's *responsibilities* and the *penalties* if the agreed requirements are not satisfied.

When a *breach of contract* occurs, and the parties in the agreement cannot agree, the *court system* steps in to settle the matter. A judge recognizes the contract as a *valid, enforceable* document.

An *ideal* contract is one where either party can honor their responsibilities. If they cannot, the court system can step in with the authority required to come to a *settlement* established by the terms of the contract or laws of the land. The *reputation* and *credibility* of the contractual parties and the court system is on the line during this process.

"For men verily swear by the greater: and an oath for confirmation is to them <u>an end of all strife</u>," (Hebrews 6:16).

What then is a *perfect* contract? One which does not have to be enforced in a court. Why? Because of the *infallible* qualities of either party in fulfilling the obligations of the contract.

God's Covenant with Abraham was *perfect*.

God gave His *promise*, and He gave His *oath*.

"Wherein God, willing more abundantly to shew unto the heirs of promise the <u>immutability of His counsel</u>, <u>confirmed it by an oath</u>:

"That by <u>two immutable things</u>, in which it was <u>impossible for God to lie</u>, we might have a strong consolation," (Hebrews 6:17-18).

Our Confidence Is In God's Character.

"That by two immutable things, in which it was impossible for God to lie, <u>we might have a strong consolation</u>, who have fled for refuge to lay hold upon the hope set before us:

"Which hope we have <u>as an anchor of the soul, both sure and stedfast</u>, and which entereth into that within the veil;

"Whither the forerunner is for us entered, <u>even Jesus, made an High Priest for ever after the order of Melchisedec</u>," (Hebrews 6:18-20).

God's Definition of Speed For Your Life

You Cannot Run Another's Race.

What is required of someone else may not be expected of you, and what is asked of you may not be demanded of someone else.

Remember Jesus' *reaction* when Peter asked about *the future* of the disciple that He loved?

"Then Peter, turning about, <u>seeth the disciple whom Jesus loved following</u>; which also leaned on His breast at supper, and said, Lord, which is he that betrayeth Thee?

"Peter seeing him saith to Jesus, Lord, and what shall this man do?

"Jesus saith unto him, If I will that he tarry till I come, <u>what is that to thee? follow thou Me</u>," (John 21:20-22).

What benefit would Peter have received from hearing about the other disciple's future? Jesus made it clear that he was to focus on Him.

Follow Thou Me

Focus On Jesus.

Rely on The Holy Spirit to *teach* you what God's definition of speed is for your life.

"Howbeit when He, the Spirit of truth, is come, <u>He will guide you into all truth</u>: for He shall not speak of Himself; but whatsoever He shall hear, that shall He speak: and <u>He will shew you things to come</u>,

"He shall glorify Me: for He shall receive of Mine, and <u>shall shew it unto you</u>.

"All things that the Father hath are Mine: therefore said I, that <u>He shall take of Mine, and shall shew it unto you</u>," (John 16:13-15).

God's definition of speed is different from yours. Whose interpretation of speed do you prefer?

God's or your own?

Heaven's speed or *man's* speed?

Supernatural speed or *natural* speed?

God's Agenda or Man's Agenda...?

It is better to follow *God's Timetable* than a timetable crafted by *wicked devices*.

"For a day in Thy courts is better than a thousand. I had <u>rather be a doorkeeper in the house of my God</u>, than to dwell in the tents of wickedness," (Psalms 84:10).

Abide in the will of God for your life, and you will *always* be on Divine Schedule. Whatever may have *fallen behind* or *off schedule* will supernaturally *realign* when you step back into His will for your life. You will never be *ashamed* when you follow God's timetable.

"And <u>I will restore to you the years</u> that the locust hath eaten, the cankerworm, and the caterpiller, and the palmerworm, My great army which I sent among you.

"And <u>ye shall eat in plenty, and be satisfied</u>, and <u>praise the name of the Lord your God</u>, that hath dealt wondrously with you: and <u>My people shall never be ashamed</u>.

"And <u>ye shall know that I am in the midst</u> of Israel, and that <u>I am the Lord your God</u>, and none else: and <u>My people shall never be ashamed</u>," (Joel 2:25-27).

Let The Light of God's Word Guide Your Steps.

"Thy word is a <u>lamp unto my feet</u>, and a <u>light unto my path</u>," (Psalm 119:105).

"The sun shall be no more thy light by day; neither for brightness shall the moon give light unto thee: but the Lord shall be <u>unto thee an Everlasting Light, and thy God thy Glory</u>.

"Thy sun shall no more go down; neither shall thy moon withdraw itself: for the Lord shall be <u>thine Everlasting Light, and the days of thy mourning shall be ended</u>," (Isaiah 60:19-20).

Trust God's Definition of Speed.

Isaiah 60:22

"A little one...

    shall become...

        a thousand...

            and a small one...

                a strong nation:

                    I the Lord...

                        will hasten it...

                            in His time."

"In His Time..."
Isaiah 60:22

~ Secret #8 ~

Trust God's Timetable

"A little one shall become a thousand, and a small one a strong nation: I the Lord will hasten it **in His time**," (Isaiah 60:22).

God's Thinking Is Different From Man's.

To understand and tap into His thinking, you need to *connect* to Him and the things of God.

"<u>Seek ye the Lord</u> while He may be found, <u>call ye upon Him</u> while He is near:

"Let the wicked forsake his way, and the unrighteous man his thoughts: and <u>let him return unto the Lord</u>, and He will have mercy upon him; and to our God, for He will abundantly pardon.

"For <u>My thoughts are not your thoughts, neither are your ways My ways</u>, saith the Lord.

"For as the <u>heavens are higher than the earth</u>, so are My ways higher than your ways, and My thoughts than your thoughts," (Isaiah 55:6-9).

Do not build your faith...your expectation...or your confidence on the *wisdom* of men...the *thinking* of men...or the *strategies* of men.

Build Your Faith In The Power of God.

"That your faith should not stand in the wisdom of men, but <u>in the power of God</u>," (1 Corinthians 2:5).

The Holy Spirit And God's Timing

As a believer, you have The Holy Spirit living *within* you. Through Him, you can *understand* the things of God.

"But as it is written, Eye hath not seen, nor ear heard, <u>neither have entered into the heart of man</u>, the things which God hath prepared for them that love Him.

"But God hath <u>revealed them unto us by His Spirit</u>: for the Spirit searcheth all things, yea, the deep things of God.

"For what man knoweth the things of a man, save the spirit of man which is in him? even so <u>the</u>

things of God knoweth no man, but <u>The Spirit of God</u>.

"Now we have received, not the spirit of the world, but The Spirit which is of God; <u>that we might know</u> the things that are freely given to us of God," (1 Corinthians 2:9-12).

"Then the angel that talked with me answered and said unto me, <u>Knowest thou not what these be</u>? And I said, No, my lord.

"Then he answered and spake unto me, saying, This is the word of the Lord unto Zerubbabel, saying, Not by might, nor by power, <u>but by My spirit</u>, saith the Lord of hosts," (Zechariah 4:5-6).

Through The Holy Spirit, we have the mind of Christ to *discern* spiritual things. Through Him, we can understand *God's timing*.

"Which things also we speak, not in the words which man's wisdom teacheth, but which <u>The Holy Ghost teacheth; comparing spiritual things with spiritual</u>.

"But <u>the natural man receiveth not</u> the things of The Spirit of God: for they are foolishness unto him: neither can he know them, because they are spiritually discerned.

"But <u>he that is spiritual judgeth all things</u>, yet he himself is judged of no man.

"For who hath known the mind of The Lord, that he may instruct Him? but <u>we have the mind of Christ</u>," (1 Corinthians 2:13-16).

Can God Say "No!" To Himself...?

According to this scripture, since we have the mind of Christ, we can *instruct* The Lord. We can petition The Lord because we will be speaking the very things that The Lord *wants* and is *interested* in doing for His Kingdom and us.

When you talk and act subject to the mind of Christ, whatever you say and do is *in* the will of God; and *advances* God's Kingdom agenda.

When You Do What God Tells You To Do And Say What God Tells You To Say, You Can Never Be Wrong.

"Thus saith the Lord, the Holy One of Israel, and his Maker, <u>Ask Me</u> of things to come concerning My sons, and <u>concerning the work of My hands command ye Me</u>," (Isaiah 45:11).

"Ask of Me, and I shall give thee the heathen for thine inheritance, and the uttermost parts of the earth for thy possession," (Psalm 2:8).

"If ye abide in Me, and My words abide in you, ye shall ask what ye will, and it shall be done unto you," (John 15:7).

Your Most Vital Connection

If you *remove* a piece of wood from the flames, it eventually becomes a *cinder*. A cinder still has *the combustible* matter in it but has *stopped* giving off flames. The cinder can be ignited but *cannot* catch fire on its own.

Why? The cinder is no longer connected.

You may have the most *expensive* smartphone money can buy. It may be the *latest* iPhone or Samsung device. If you do not have a network or internet service, your device is *severely restricted* in its capacity. Certain features of the device are wholly *unavailable* or *unusable*.

Why? The device is no longer connected.

Your *spiritual* life works in the same way. You will never be able to attain the *full potential* of what

God created you for without having a *connection* with your Creator.

Sin cut us off from Him.

Jesus died and rose again that our connection may be *restored*. Your connection to Him enables all other things that pertain to your life and greatness to be added to you.

"For God so loved the world, that He gave His only begotten Son, <u>that whosoever believeth in Him should not perish, but have everlasting life</u>," (John 3:16).

Your Greatness Is On God's Mind

Jesus Is Your Most Vital Connection.

"I am <u>the True Vine</u>..." (John 15:1).

An encounter with Jesus is the most *vital* connection any human being will ever have. Your attachment to Him *preserves* your timing.

God is interested in your *productivity*.

"I am the True Vine, and <u>My Father is the Husbandman.</u>

"Every branch in Me that beareth not fruit He taketh away: and <u>every branch that beareth fruit, He purgeth it, that it may bring forth more fruit</u>" (John 15:1-2).

He schedules "pruning" for every branch that it may be more productive. Have *confidence* in His process. Have *faith* in His timing. What He speaks over you, *sanctifies* and *cleanses* you on your journey in Greatness.

Listen Attentively To Divine Instructions.

Listen Attentively To Divine Correction.

"Now <u>ye are clean</u> through the word which <u>I have spoken unto you</u>," (John 15:3).

You Are Nothing Without Him

You Cannot Have God-Results Without God.

"Abide in Me, and I in you. As <u>the branch cannot bear fruit of itself</u>, except it abide in the vine; no more can ye, except ye abide in Me.

"I am The Vine, ye are the branches: He that abideth in Me, and I in him, <u>the same bringeth forth much fruit: for without Me ye can do nothing</u>.

"If a man abide not in Me, he is cast forth as a branch, and is withered; and men gather them, and cast them into the fire, and they are burned," (John 15:4-6).

Your connection to God *secures* your Greatness and *preserves* your timing.

God is glorified in your Greatness.

"If ye abide in Me, and My words abide in you, ye shall ask what ye will, and it shall be done unto you.

"Herein is My Father glorified, that ye bear much fruit; so shall ye be My disciples," (John 15:7-8).

It Is Not What It Looks Like

When you abide in Him, what may *initially* appear as a failure is concealing your *greatest* victories.

Samson receiving a haircut looked like failure... *yet more Philistines died at the time of his death than killed during his lifetime.*

"And Samson said, Let me die with the Philistines. And he bowed himself with all his might; and the house fell upon the lords, and upon all the people that were therein. <u>So the dead which he slew at his death were more than they which he slew in his life,</u>" (Judges 16:30).

Joseph, being thrown in prison, looked like a failure...*yet that was the path to becoming Prime Minister.* (See Genesis 40-41.)

"And Pharaoh said unto his servants, Can we find such a one as this is, <u>a man in whom the Spirit of God is</u>?

"And Pharaoh said unto Joseph, Forasmuch as God hath shewed thee all this, <u>there is none so discreet and wise as thou art</u>:

"Thou shalt be over my house, and according unto thy word shall all my people be ruled: <u>only in the throne will I be greater than thou,</u>" (Genesis 41:38-40).

Jesus' limp body on The Cross looked like failure...yet the scripture says, "for had they known it, <u>they would not have crucified the Lord of glory,</u>" (1 Corinthians 2:8).

The Divine Timing Paradox

At the time of God's visitation, that moment of manifestation, when our faith connects the earth realm with our Divine release...

...every loss becomes a *gain*...

...every failure turns into *success*...

...every betrayal ultimately inspires *loyalty*...

...every false accusation ends up in *promotion*.

All Shame Evaporates At God's Timing.

"And <u>I will restore to you the years</u> that the locust hath eaten, the cankerworm, and the caterpiller, and the palmerworm, My great army which I sent among you.

"And ye shall eat in plenty, and be satisfied, and praise the name of the Lord your God, that hath dealt wondrously with you: and <u>My people shall never be ashamed.</u>

"And ye shall know that I am in the midst of Israel, and that I am the Lord your God, and none else: and <u>My people shall never be ashamed,</u>" (Joel 2:25-27).

Stay Conscious of The Rewards of God's Timing

Do not act in a way that would *sabotage* your schedule or *stain* your testimony. Make the most of every opportunity God sends your way.

Your journey in Greatness is *on display*, even to those who do not know The Lord.

"Walk in wisdom toward them that are without, redeeming the time," (Colossians 4:5).

The worldly timetable is compassed by stealing, killing, and destroying. God's timetable ultimately produces restoration, healing, and visitation. *God's plan is framed with life and that "more abundantly."*

"The thief cometh not, but for to steal, and to kill, and to destroy: I am come that they might have life, and that they might have it more abundantly," (John 10:10).

Yielding to God's timetable may be difficult, but the results are *assured*. Let Him *work* in you what needs to be worked. Let Him *change* in you what needs to be changed. Let Him *cultivate* in you a way of *living* and *mindset* of right standing with Him that seeks *harmony* with His will and purpose.

"Now no chastening for the present seemeth to be joyous, but grievous: nevertheless <u>afterward it yieldeth the peaceable fruit of righteousness</u> unto them which are exercised thereby," (Hebrews 12:11).

God's Timetable Delivers A Great Inheritance.

"Thy people also shall be all righteous: <u>they shall inherit the land for ever</u>, the branch of My planting, the work of My hands, <u>that I may be glorified</u>.

"A little one shall become a thousand, and a small one a strong nation: I the Lord will hasten it **in His time**," (Isaiah 60:21-22).

Your Greatness glorifies God.

Trust God's Timetable.

Conclusion

On your journey, you will find yourself developing in your Greatness, not because it is popular with everyone, but because you know *it is the right thing to do*. Then as you educate people on the importance of their own development, they too will become ignited.

Do not get *sidetracked* or *discouraged* by people who are not where you are. Never *apologize* about nor regret who and what God has made you to be. Each person must develop along their journey in Greatness. You cannot do it for them.

Do not give people what they want; give people *what The Lord anoints you to offer*. Never limit yourself to what people expect; *expand yourself into what God wants you to be*.

There will always be *more* in your heart when you represent God than what people are *ready* for or *can handle*. Jesus even said to His disciples, "you cannot bear all that I have for you."

Instead, He relied on The Holy Spirit to *prepare* the disciples.

"I have yet many things to say unto you, <u>but ye cannot bear them now</u>.

"Howbeit when He, the Spirit of truth, is come, <u>He will guide you</u> into all truth: for He shall not speak of Himself; but whatsoever He shall hear, that shall He speak: and <u>He will shew you things to come</u>," (John 16:12-13).

Stay true to your journey in Greatness, and let The Lord *intervene* in the lives of those who may not understand what you must do to get there.

Greatness Is A Never-Ending Journey.

May The Lord help you become **a thousand**, may The Lord help you become **a strong nation**; may **The Lord hasten you in His time**.

Great Grace To You On Your Journey!

YOUR KINGDOM INVITATION

The Lord Jesus is the King of kings and The Lord of lords. When you *receive* Him and decide to live a life that *glorifies* Him, you *become* a part of His glorious Kingdom. You access your Greatness!

"But seek ye first the kingdom of God, and His righteousness; and all these things shall be added unto you," (Matthew 6:33).

"For whosoever shall call upon the name of the Lord shall be saved," (Romans 10:13).

Decide to live for Him.

Accept your Kingdom *invitation* today.

"That if thou shalt confess with thy mouth the Lord Jesus, and shalt believe in thine heart that God hath raised Him from the dead, thou shalt be saved. For with the heart man believeth unto righteousness; and with the mouth confession is made unto salvation," (Romans 10:9-10).

Pray this prayer today.

"Lord Jesus, I believe that You died for me. I believe that You rose from the dead. I believe You can save me. I acknowledge I am a sinner. I need You in my life. I want to follow You. I want to serve You. Come into my heart. Forgive my sins. I receive eternal life with You. Fill me with your Precious Holy Spirit. I dedicate my life to You. I choose to live the rest of my life for You. In Jesus' Name. Amen!"

If you prayed that prayer and received our Lord Jesus Christ as your personal Savior, please let us know. Also, please let us know how this book touched your life.

Connect with us at **8GreatSecrets.com**

About The Author

Paul J Nyamweya is an entrepreneur with a passion for helping people be the best version of themselves. His passion is to help leaders lead leaders, and teachers teach teachers.

Paul has had over ten years of experience as a Project Management Professional. He has received formal education on three different continents; Africa, Europe, and North America. Paul possesses a comprehensive background as a consultant, project manager, and sales professional credited with combining creative options and expertise to deliver cost-effective design options and solutions. He has completed over 100 projects of varying scope and complexity.

Paul has extensive experience in Construction, Media & Publishing, and Insurance. He holds a Bachelor's and Master's degree in Architecture. He currently resides in the Dallas/Fort Worth Metroplex, where he also serves in ministry.

www.ingramcontent.com/pod-product-compliance
Lightning Source LLC
Chambersburg PA
CBHW071959090426
42740CB00011B/2013